GET THE MONKEY OFF YOUR BACK

How to Deal With the Financial Services Industry

COOPER PEEL

ISBN: 1499255861
ISBN 13: 9781499255867
Library of Congress Control Number: 2014907952
CreateSpace Independent Publishing Platform
North Charleston, South Carolina

TABLE OF CONTENTS

Introduction 1

What Mutual Funds Really Cost 3

Buy and Hold 5

Dollar Cost Averaging...6

How to Beat 75 Percent
of Mutual Funds..7

Berkshire Hathaway...8

Berkshire Hathaway Instead of an Annuity
or Mutual Fund 9

How Can the Adverage Joe or Jane Do to Beat
the Professional Investors 11

Conference With Your Accountant........................... 11

Trust Funds 12

Advice to Young People.. 12

Get It In Writing.. 13

What Are Your Friends Doing 13

Day Trading 13

Living Too Much for Today vs. Too Much for Tomorrow 13

How to Spot a Gimic 14

Depression Mentality 14

Form 990 14

Retirement Options 15

No Sales Charge... 17

Really Dumb 18

Don't Have The time 18

Captive Investments 19

Where Mutual Funds Spend Most of Their Money.................. 20

Unit Trust 20

Too Good To Be True.. 22

Financial Advice on The Internet... 22

Rental Property.. 22

Doctor and The Cows.. 23

Cheating on Taxes 24

Cell Phone Tower..24

Passive Investing.. 25

Bonds and Interst Rates 26

Buy and Hold Etf Or Stock Instead Of An Annuity 27

Annuity Hole 29

Life Insurance... 29

Whole Life or Buy Term And Invest The Difference 32

Avoid The Life Insurance Salesperson 33

Group Life Insurance 34

How Much Life Insurance Do I Need? 34

Nobody Ever Lost Money With Life Insurance 35

Resort Property.. 35

Home and Auto Insurance.. 36

Umbrella 37

How Great are The Brokerage Firms? 37

Is Having An Asset Model Worth 1 Percent A Year?............... 38

Tax Inefficiency... 38

Managed Etfs 42

Why Can't The Financial Services Industry Charge
By The Hour Like Lawyers And Accountants? 42

I Will Manage Your 401K For 1/2 Percent............................ 43

Surrender Charges 43

Old National Geographics 44

Investments That Imply That You Can
Always Get Your Money Back... 44

Investments That Imply That You Can't Lose Money.............. 45

Seminars With Free Dinners 45

Walk Away At The First Hint Of Dishonesty........................ 46

Closed-In Reits 46

Simplicity..47

Lunch For Idiots 47

Liquidity 47

Varible Life Insurance 47

Fifty-Second Birthday.. 48

The Man Above Marilyn Monroe.................................... 49

Box Of Rocks 49

Selling Something That You Don't Know The Value Of........... 50

Ious And Cosighned Loans 50

Set Up Your Estate To Avoid Probate 51

Patience...51

Knowing When To Take A Loss......................................51

Chasing Winners..51

Tax Efficient 52

Invest In Companies That Make Things
People Must Have.. 52

Things That Advisors Won't Tell You...................... 53

The Way Things Used To Be 53

Time-Share 54

Capital Gains Rate.. 54

The Best Real Estate Investment:your Office 55

Shared Vacation Homes 55

What Percent Should I Invest In Stocks? 55

Leverage.. 56

Disability Plan... 57

Gold... 57

Lottery... 58

Other Peoples Money.. 59

Excess Money In Life Insurance Policy 59

Take Loss To Cover Windfall 60

Exchange Funds 60

Bond Swap 61

College Savings.. 61

Buy And Don't Be Sold 63

Ask Old Investors About Their Limited
Partnership Experiences... 64

How Pension Funds And Insurance
Companies Invest Their Money 66

Never.. 66

If You Don't Want Your Kids To Get Along
After You Are Gone 67

He Even Died In 1974 67

Best Manager Out Of Many 68

Last Dollar 69

Stick By The Rules 69

Partnerships 69

Long-Term Care Insurance 70

Self Insured Vs. No Insurance 72

Don't Be Insurance Poor 73

"Don't Leave Your 401K At Your Old Job" 73

Professions That Are Bad With Money 73

How To Deal With Your Financial Advisor 74

Don't Need A Financial Advisor 75

Social Security 75

Generosity 76

Expectations 76

Throwing Darts 76

People Who Always Get In The Market At The High 77

Heated Stock Market 77

When To Sell 77

Mail Box 78

Basis 78

A Really Bad Investment, Lidigation 78

Portfolio Of Core Stocks 78

Play Money 79

Your Friends At The Bank 79

Learn From Others Mistakes 80

Pick Five Show-Offs In Your Town.. 80

Where Are The Real Brokers 81

Corporate Bonds 81

Municipal Bonds 82

Am I Being Too Greedy?... 82

How To Find The Low 82

Other Peoples Hands 83

Everybody And Their Brother
Or Sister In The Financial
Services Industry 83

Managed Money... 84

When To Convert To A Roth.. 85

When To Roth Instead Of Pre- Tax Contributions.................... 86

They Are Treating People Like Idiots At The Bank 86

Nonprofits 87

Make Your Own Mutual Fund.. 87

25.65 Percent In Expenses Over Ten Years To
Underperform An Index 89

Making Bad Investment Decisions In Order To
Save On Taxes 89

The Goverment Will Need More Money In The Future............ 90

The Power Of Deffered Income 90

The Boys At Jackass... 90

House Vs. Condo 91

How Could They Hide My 401K Fees For Eighteen Years Without Me Knowing?.. 91

Don't Take No For An Answer 92

4 Percent Rate Of Return 92

Travel 93

Biggest Travel Mistakes 93

Travel Tips 93

Glossary 97

INTRODUCTION

I WROTE THIS BOOK to help the individual investor learn how to think for themselves and control the costs of their investments. This isn't a too good to be true or a can't lose money book. Most financial books are written by salespeople, academics, or journalist. I am an average Joe who was in the financial services industry long enough to know all of the tricks.

"From 1980 to 2006, the US financial Service Sector grew from 4.9 percent to 8.3 percent of GDP. A substantial share of that increase represented increases in asset management fees." The financial services industry is working for itself, not for you. In the old days, people bought individual stocks and bonds and held them for the long term without annual fees. Brokers earned their money. Today, the financial services industry wants to put all of your investments into captive products, or charge you an annual fee on your whole account.

This book will show you the products that you should demand from your financial advisor. Your investments should not cost over one fourth of a percent a year (25 basis points) and they should be tax efficient and simple. If you buy and hold low cost ETFs or stocks from an advisor and hold them for an average of twelve years, your annual cost should not exceed this amount.

If you pay 2 percent instead of 1/4 percent a year on your investments, you will have 1/3 less on a lump sum after 25 years, or half after 42 years, assuming a 7 percent rate of return.

I grew up in the 1960s in rural Eastern North Carolina. People in those days lived and invested modestly. Many owned farm and timberland. They bought blue chip, or local stocks, or bonds that they understood and held for the long term. Mutual funds were affordable, unlike today. They spent way less on financial services. Only those who were able to pay cash owned resort property. The only captive investment that they owned was life insurance.

Vanguard started in 1974, introducing low cost index funds, which outperformed the managed accounts mainly because of low fees and expenses. You would think that the industry would have become more competitive, but instead it has gotten worse. People are paying way more on their investments today than they should.

I wrote this book to help the individual investor think for themselves, stay out of trouble, and control expenses. I learned a lot from being in the financial services industry in the1980s and from my investment experience. I am not an expert, but there are very few people who would not benefit from reading this book, including the so-called professionals, most of whom are just salespeople.

Burton G Malkie, You're Paying Too Much for Investment Help, Wall Street Journal, May 28,2013

WHAT MUTUAL FUNDS REALLY COST

MUTUAL FUNDS COST MUCH more, and they make you much less than they would like you to believe.

Most mutual funds cost around 2 percent a year, plus sales charges. The annual expenses are only part of the cost. Don't let an advisor confuse you into believing that the annual expenses are the true annual cost. If you are unable to determine the true annual cost, then use a 2 percent assumption.

To determine the cost of a mutual fund you must add the annual expenses, sales charges, maintenance fees, 12B-1 fees, and additional expenses. The annual expenses are easy to find in the annual report. The sales charges, unless you pay at purchase, can be very confusing. Many people don't think that they are paying deferred sales charges, when they are. If your mutual fund has surrender charges, then you are paying deferred sales charges. The maintenance fee is paid from your account to the firm that holds your mutual funds and is usually 1/4 percent (25 basis points). You are much smarter than I am if you can find where the maintenance fee is taken from your account. The 12 B-1 fees that many funds have are for advertizing the fund in order to make the fund larger, in order to reduce expenses, which never happens. The statement of additional information which you must request shows items that are not covered by your annual expenses. Before writing this book I thought, like everybody else, that commissions were covered in the annual expenses, not in the additional expenses, which aren't disclosed unless requested.

The mutual fund companies own the brokerage firms that they use for trades, which they don't disclose unless you request the statement of additional expenses. The average mutual fund spends 16 million a year on commissions, costing an extra 1/2 to 3/4 percent that most people, including most advisors are unaware of. They consider that relationship to be ethical, but I don't, and I doubt that you would either. Life is too short for me, and also for most financial advisors, to try and figure out the true cost of a mutual fund. I do know that they cost too much. Unless you are willing to spend hours trying to figure out the true cost, you should not be invested in them. Never invest in any investment unless you know the true cost. Never invest in any investment that has the ability to overcharge you without you being able to figure it out.

The average mutual fund costs around 2 percent a year. The doctor and the cows and other people's hands on your money chapters are examples of how investors that are not savvy get treated. Why would anyone be in an investment when they don't have a clue as to what they are being charged? My advice to invest in things that are real, without annual fees or expenses makes even more sense after you figure out that you have been getting ripped off.

The history of the mutual fund companies is simple. They got greedy over time.

"The generally poor performance of funds relative to the market is not due to the fact that managers of these funds pick losing stocks. Their performance lags the benchmarks largely because funds impose fees and trading costs that average 2 percent per year."

Another disadvantage of mutual funds is the extra cost incurred when buying large blocks of stocks or in down markets when shares have to be sold in order to cover investors that sell shares.

I just say no to packaged investments and don't invest my money in any product that would take hours to figure out the true cost. How much control do you have if you can't figure out the true cost of your investments? The financial services industry hasn't figured out a way to hide expenses from buy and hold stock and bond investors.

Stocks For The Long Run, Jeremy J Siegel, McGraw Hill, New York, 2002, page 349

BUY AND HOLD

IF YOU LEARN ONLY one thing from this book, it is that that buy and hold works. It always did. Buy and hold is a time proven strategy of buying quality stocks or ETFs that you know and understand and holding them for the long term. Buy and hold is very tax efficient since you only pay taxes on the dividends, which are taxed a lower rate. Holding investments with a long term approach is much less costly and risky than accounts that trade often. Berkshire Hathaway is an example of what a successful buy and hold strategy can accomplish.

Financial advisors are trained to talk you out of buy and hold, just as I was when I was an EF Hutton broker. There is not much in it for them if you do this with your portfolio. If an advisor tries to talk you out of buy and hold, find another advisor. If an advisor tries to talk you into captive products, you are better off without them. No advice is better than advice from a greedy advisor.

Lately, some advisors have gotten away with charging an annual fee to buy and hold investors. I recently read an article in *Barons* about an advisor who charges annual fees on everything including long-term bonds. A 1 percent annual fee on a fifteen-year bond would cost 15 percent over the life of the bond instead of a 1.5 percent sales charge, which is the most the customer should have paid. Even the original low-cost brokerage firm has a program for those willing to pay 1 percent a year on their investments. Nobody in the old days would believe that people would actually be paying for bottled water or paying annual fees on their investments.

Everyone in the financial services industry wants you to think that they are giving proven (old-fashioned) advice; but the truth is they are charging the customer much more than they did in the old days, while creating more taxable events due to higher turnover.

Buy and hold works even better today with ETFs.

DOLLAR COST AVERAGING

DOLLAR COST AVERAGING IS a buy and hold strategy. Over time you buy more shares of stock when prices are low and less when prices are high. Dollar cost averaging is also a good way to not let your emotions lose you money. Your emotions, if you are not careful, will have you buy when the market is high and sell when the market is low.

HOW TO BEAT 75 PERCENT OF MUTUAL FUNDS

INVEST IN LOW-COST BROAD-BASED ETFs, and you will beat the performance of over 75 percent of mutual funds and money managers over time. You can get a low cost broad based ETF for as low as five basis points per year, whereas the average mutual fund costs around 2 percent a year. Two percent a year is 28.5 percent of your profit if the market does 7 percent, which a reasonable rate of return to expect over time. The market has done around 7 percent for the last 200 years. Last year's 32.4 percent return on the S&P 500 is even more reason to expect modest returns in the future. Five basis points cost you a little more than seven-tenths of a percent if the market does 7 percent. I call this the roll over and play dead strategy because you've given up on outsmarting the market while beating the performance of over 75 percent of mutual funds and money managers. You also save on taxes, due to less account turnover. When I was young, this did not appeal to me because I felt that I could easily beat the market. After years of investing, I have been humbled enough to realize that plans that are too good to be true usually don't work. I may not beat the market, but I can control my costs, and to a large extent, my taxes. There are many indexes or ETFs from which to choose. They even have ETFs designed to charge you too much. One captive insurance company, which charges too much for insurance, has an S&P 500 ETF that costs seventy-six basis points, over fifteen times more than a low cost S&P 500 ETF should cost.

ETFs are much more tax efficient than accounts that trade often. With an ETF, you only pay taxes on the dividends, which are taxed at a preferred rate. Less fees and less taxes equals more money for you.

BERKSHIRE HATHAWAY

IF THE FINANCIAL SERVICES industry was so great, then why didn't they recommend Berkshire Hathaway to their customers?

When a mutual fund gets too big, it is considered to be a disadvantage. The larger Berkshire gets, the more ability it has to buy companies or take advantage of opportunities such as the GE, Bank of America, and Goldman Sachs 10% convertible preferred shares that Berkshire bought after the correction in 2009. You and I, or your mutual funds or money managers, were unable to take advantage of these deals.

Use the compound-interest-rate calculator from the Internet to see how much more money you could potentially have over time without paying 2 percent a year in unnecessary fees to the financial services industry.

An investment doesn't get any more tax efficient than Berkshire Hathaway. No dividend equals no IRS Form 1099 or any taxable event unless you sell.

Berkshire Hathaway was 12 dollars a share in 1965 and over 220,000 dollars a share in 2015.

There are people who invest everything they have in Berkshire Hathaway. They have done very well, and are well positioned for the future. I would much rather have all of my investments in Berkshire than in overpriced mutual funds or managed money.

Always ask yourself if you would not mind holding an investment during a correction before investing. I cannot think of a better stock to own during a correction or recession than Berkshire Hathaway.

BERKSHIRE HATHAWAY INSTEAD OF AN ANNUITY OR MUTUAL FUND

THE AVERAGE MUTUAL FUND costs 2 percent a year. Why not have a Berkshire position instead. Having one less 1099, and no taxable event at tax season would be as good as it gets if you are investing for growth.

The average variable annuity costs between 2.5 to 3.5 percent a year in fees and expenses. They are well hidden in order to keep you, the customer, fat, dumb, and happy. Most advisors who like selling annuities avoid mentioning the fees and expenses to their customers. Most advisors don't understand the cost structure, but they all know exactly what they make selling them. Annuities would not be very popular if people knew what they cost, or if they understood the tax disadvantages. If you invest $10,000 in Berkshire Hathaway and hold it for thirty years, at an 8 percent yield, you would have $107,651 compared to $38,284 with the annuity that costs 3.5 percent a year in annual fees, assuming it had the same rate of return as the Berkshire before expenses. Who is getting rich: you or the financial service industry?

How can so many financial advisors sell things based on tax savings that just aren't there? Berkshire, like all long-term stocks or ETFs, smokes the annuity with its tax advantages. Both defer income since Berkshire pays no dividend. Deferral of income is the main selling point of the annuity. The Berkshire has no annual fees or expenses, unlike the annuity, which is wrapped up with fees and expenses that are extremely difficult to find. Berkshire has no surrender charges and has complete liquidity, unlike the annuity. With the annuity, the first dollar out is taxed as ordinary income, unless you annuitize your payments. If your annuity is invested in stocks, you lose the tax break that the IRS allows for dividends and capital gains. With Berkshire, only the gain is taxable when shares are sold, and then at a preferred capital gains rate, which is in most cases 13 percent lower than the ordinary income rate at which the annuity is taxed. At death, whoever inherits the stock gets a stepped up basis. They could sell it without any income taxes. With the annuity, the spouse gets no tax break except for the continued deferral of the account. With the annuity, when left to heirs, the taxes on the gains must be paid as ordinary income in that year. With stock, you also have the ability to gift shares to others. The annuity has absolutely no tax advantage over stocks or ETFs, except for the deferral of income. As long as Berkshire doesn't pay a dividend, it defers income much better than the variable annuity.

I guarantee that when you hear the financial services industry advertizing *the power of deferred income*, they are not talking about Berkshire Hathaway or any buy and hold strategy. The financial services industry is trying to take you for a ride, the annuity ride, which has been very profitable for them and very mediocre for the investor.

As an investor, your portfolio would be much better off with a Berkshire Hathaway position. If your 401K allows for you to invest in individual stocks, why not put a percentage of it in Berkshire. This would greatly reduce the mutual fund fees that are taking a serious bite out of your retirement. Do you have any idea how much your 401K is costing you in fees and expenses over your lifetime? You should.

I always laugh when I see an account designed by a so called professional that doesn't have a Berkshire Hathaway position.

HOW CAN THE ADVERAGE JOE OR JANE DO TO BEAT THE PROFESSIONAL INVESTORS

YOU THE INVESTOR HAVE a 2 percent advantage a year over mutual funds, since you are getting to save the 2 percent that you would be paying in fees and expenses. If the stock market does 7 percent over time, a 2 percent savings would be an enormous advantage. If you look at the largest holdings of most mutual funds, you will mostly find core stocks. How difficult is it to pick core stocks (leaders in their industries) that have a good dividend history, and hold on to them for the long term? You are not going to get rich investing in core stocks, but you are not going to lose your ass either. Have a plan to never panic sell, and buy if able, when a correction takes place.

One advantage that you have over the professional investor is that you will not get fired over poor short term results. Your investments should be for the long term.

Professional investors on average underperform the market after expenses.

If this strategy is not suitable for you, consider a low cost, broad based ETF for your investment needs.

CONFERENCE WITH YOUR ACCOUNTANT

A CONFERENCE WITH YOUR accountant is a valuable tool for your financial planning. Their advice will help keep you out of trouble, since they have seen many, if not all of the mistakes that investors make. Always check with your accountant before taking a large capital gain to see if you can save on taxes by taking the gain over a number of years, if able. Tax season is too late for planning, with the exception of IRA contributions. Always check with your accountant before buying any financial product that you think might be overpriced or too good to be true. Financial advisors that like selling overpriced packaged products hate to make presentations in front of accountants. Life insurance salespeople won't insult your intelligence in front of an accountant either.

TRUST FUNDS

IF YOU ARE LEAVING a large estate to heirs, consider a trust fund. Chapters 5 and 6 of *The Millionaire Next Door, by Thomas J Stanley and William D Danko* should be required reading for those leaving a substantial amount of money to their children. If you have an adult child that is dependent on your financial support, you don't have a choice.

ADVICE TO YOUNG PEOPLE

YOUNG PEOPLE TODAY CANNOT afford to make mistakes with their investments since their opportunities will be less. Stocks, bonds, real estate, jobs, and Social Security will not be as lucrative as it was for my generation. The stock market, which over the last 200 years averaged 7 percent, will probably return closer to its average. Bonds with today's low interest rates, offer very little. Home ownership will not be nearly as profitable, especially for those who have to move often. Jobs will be more competitive, and most retirement plans will be 401K instead of pensions. Some states are even considering 401K retirement plans. Social Security will end up costing the young more, while they get less. The only thing positive might be lower inflation.

GET IT IN WRITING

DON'T EVER MAKE AN offer on real estate unless you have a contract ready for the seller to sign. A verbal agreement is just as binding as a written one, it's just much more difficult to prove. People, especially family and friends, tend to have second thoughts after making an unsigned agreement. Realtors always get a contract in writing quickly as possible. So should you.

WHAT ARE YOUR FRIENDS DOING

DO YOUR OWN THINKING about your investments. A proven way to lose money is to blindly follow the advice of friends, family, co-workers, and many times advisors.

DAY TRADING

IF DAY TRADING WAS a proven way to make money, the institutions on Wall Street would be doing it. Day trading is a proven way to lose money and create stress.

LIVING TOO MUCH FOR TODAY VS. TOO MUCH FOR TOMORROW

YOU NEED BALANCE WITH your savings/spending habits. Not saving enough for the future is clearly a mistake. Saving too much for the future and not enjoying things that you should have in order for your children to be better off can also be a mistake.

HOW TO SPOT A GIMIC

EVERYBODY WANTS SOMETHING FOR nothing. All gimmicks are based on the assumption that the buyer will be greedy. If something seems like it is too good to be true, it probably is.

DEPRESSION MENTALITY

MY PARENTS GENERATION HAD the depression mentality. They did not believe in borrowing money unless necessary. If you drive a luxury automobile, then you should be able to pay cash for it. You should never own a home that you cannot afford, even if it is going up in value. They believed that paying off a home loan was better than having a loan and investing the difference, even if the market outperformed the interest on the loan over time. Depression mentality is out of style today, but it looked mighty good in 2009.

FORM 990

THE NEXT TIME YOU get a call from a charity that you know little about, ask them to send you a copy of their IRS form 990, which shows where the money goes. You have the right to choose your own charities.

RETIREMENT OPTIONS

NEVER BUY TERM LIFE insurance to cover your spouse instead of taking the joint and survivor option on your retirement plan, which provides lifetime benefits for your spouse.

If you buy 25 times the spousal benefit in permanent insurance, then your spouse will be adequately covered. Your investments would have to return 4 percent in order not to deplete this amount. For planning purposes always use a conservative 4 percent rate of return. Living off 4 percent a year was considered to be a sure way to preserve the principal until recently when interest rates hit record lows. The insurance in most cases will cost more, but it could be worth more if you live to an old age.

With most retirement plans, including Social Security, all of the options are actuarially the same amount of money. Don't gamble in order to get more income. Beating the system by buying life insurance doesn't work unless the joint and survivor benefit is worth less money. Don't ever have an advisor or life insurance salesperson sell you on a lump sum option without having it looked over by your accountant first. Your accountant doesn't stand to gain by you taking the lump sum option. Make the advisor or life insurance salesperson do their presentation in front of your accountant, to keep it honest.

A lump sum, such as a retirement buyout, is like a worm on a hook to a greedy financial advisor. The corporation that is offering you the lump sum understands the time value of money much better than you or your advisor. The only advantage that you might have over the company would be if you or your spouse were in bad health. Some advisers will tell you that they can do better over time with the lump sum than the retirement benefit would provide. Don't let an advisor use the trick of showing you a high assumption in order to sell you on the lump sum option. If these advisors were so great, then maybe they should manage money for the big corporations who apparently don't understand the time value of money. The lump sum is actuarially the same amount of money as the other retirement options. If an advisor uses a high assumption, then taking the lump sum would look very attractive. Always look at the worst case when considering taking the lump sum option. Don't let an advisor use a high assumption, unless you have enough assets to gamble. Not all corrections recovered as quickly as the last one. Use a 4 percent assumption to be safe, unless you can take afford to take the risk. If you had retired in 1974, 4.4 percent is the most that you could have taken from a balanced account without running out of money. Do you want a retirement plan that would have run out of money if you had retired at the worst time in the last 60 years? An advisor that gets to invest your lump sum will make a lot of money from your conversion, and nothing if you keep your pension. The advisors that will talk you into the lump sum option will put you in mutual funds or managed money, costing you way more than the big corporations pay to invest their money. Why would anyone want advice, even though it is supposedly free, from someone with that much of a conflict of interest? Always meet with your accountant who does not stand to gain from your decision before considering the lump sum option.

If you have any doubts about the future ability of the company providing the retirement, then a lump sum would make sense. If you have enough excess net worth to afford to be fully invested in the market in your retirement years, then investing the lump sum could pay off. If you cannot afford to have your retirement in the market during a correction, you should not consider the lump sum option.

Inflation must be considered with your retirement planning. If your pension doesn't have cost of living increases then you must save or have money from other sources to make up for inflation. Even today's modest inflation could greatly reduce the buying power if you live long enough.

NO SALES CHARGE

IF YOU ARE TOLD by an advisor that an investment doesn't have a sales charge, that should be your red flag. I only know of one investment that does not have a sales charge to the customer: newly issued municipal bonds. The issuer of the bonds pay the sales charges. Investments that don't honestly disclose sales charges, you do not want. They are by far the most expensive. Always look at the surrender charges to get an idea of what the expenses are. Closed- end REITs don't have surrender charges, since they take 15 percent off of the top. Closed- End REITs have an artificial value that makes you think that they are worth what you are paying for them. I have a simple rule to avoid trouble: never buy investments without a sales charge or with a surrender charge. If you are told that a packaged investment doesn't have a sales charges, it is your responsibility to report the advisor to the state regulators for fraud.

If you and only invest in things that are real, that are worth what you pay for them, minus a reasonable sales charge that is honestly disclosed, you want get ripped off.

REALLY DUMB

1. Co-signing a loan
2. Loaning money to family and friends
3. Trying to collect money from family and friends
4. Buying a time-share
5. Buying a lottery ticket
6. Not having disability insurance if you need the income
7. Not knowing how much you are paying for financial services
8. Not having adequate life insurance
9. Buying an annuity in order to save on taxes
10. Putting off buying life insurance

DON'T HAVE THE TIME

IF YOU DON'T HAVE the time to pay attention to your investments, then you should invest in a low cost broad based ETF with a buy and hold approach. Don't be talked into mutual funds that cost 2 percent a year unless you plan on working several more years in order to pay them. Do not panic and sell when corrections take place. You will do better than 75 percent of mutual funds or money managers over time, if not more. You will also pay much less in taxes on taxable accounts with this strategy.

Always use an independent insurance agent, or if you don't then shop your insurance to make sure that you are paying a competitive rate with your captive agent. If you add up your home, auto, umbrella, health, disability and life insurance, you will find insurance to be one of your largest expenses. Consider higher deductibles as a way to reduce cost. Remember that with the higher deductable you should file fewer claims, making your insurance score higher. Always have an umbrella policy. Get adequate disability insurance and more than enough life insurance to cover your needs. Get your own life insurance policy instead of group life insurance through work. Schedule a meeting with your accountant to discuss planning issues with your next year's tax review.

Very few people would be better off without an advisor. That doesn't mean to let others do your thinking for you unless you plan on being poorer in your old age.

CAPTIVE INVESTMENTS

THE FINANCIAL SERVICES INDUSTRY would like for all of your investments to be captive. They make a lot more from you with captive investments. The only captive investments that I own are low cost ETFs. I always know the cost of all my investments. One reason that I don't own mutual funds is that I am too lazy to figure out the cost. The other reason is that I don't like being ripped off. The financial services industry wants to have their hands all over your money. With stocks, bonds, and low cost ETFs, they don't make anything unless you buy or sell. Annuities, limited partnerships, closed-end REITs, variable life insurance, high cost ETFs (ETFs that cost much more than they should), mutual funds, etc, they end up making a monkey out of you. They will turn your whole account into a captive investment if you are dumb enough to be talked into paying an annual fee. They make more while you, the customer, makes less: it's that simple.

WHERE MUTUAL FUNDS SPEND MOST OF THEIR MONEY

MUTUAL FUNDS SPEND A pittance on research compared to the amount that they spend on advertising.

UNIT TRUST

WHEN I WAS A broker in the late 1980s, I saw many disappointed customers that had invested in the NC Municipal Bond Unit Trust. They had purchased these in order to take advantage of high interest rates a few years earlier. The unit trust contained newly issued bonds that had high interest payments, but with a 2 to 3 percent call feature.(A call feature is when the issuer of the bonds can buy the bondholders out at a small premium if they want, usually to their advantage.) They were trying to take advantage of the high interest rates the wrong way. They were all disappointed because their bonds were called when interest rates went down. The Unit Trust paid 4 percent (hidden, or not easily disclosed) commission instead of the normal 1.5 percent for newly issued bonds. The unit trust investors were automatically put in the NC municipal bond mutual fund that was paying around 3.5 percent when the bonds were called.

With bonds, they win or you lose. If interest rates go up, you are stuck with an investment that is worth less money, even though you will get your money back at maturity. If interest rates go down, making your bonds worth more money, they can pay you a small call premium and walk away. With discounted bonds on the secondary market, you are protected if a decrease in interest rates occurs. At the present, rates are so low that discounted bonds would not exist, except for issuers with bad or unsure credit.

I had a client who bought only secondary bonds, which because of the high interest rates at the time were selling for forty to sixty cents on the dollar. The coupons(interest payments) were much smaller. His coupons were tax free, but the discount on the bonds were taxable. He was still making 10 to 12 percent on his bonds that he bought long after the customers who used brokers that sold them the NC Municipal Bond Unit Trust were settling for 3.5 percent in the mutual fund. The lesson here is that the investor who can think for themselves will do much better that those who don't. The lesson here for advisors is that when you make 4 percent instead of 1.5 percent it can't be good for the customer.

This is just one example of why getting free advice from a financial advisor who makes money selling you products is not in your best interest. None of my client's bonds were called, but if they had been, he would have made a substantial profit on the call since all of his bonds were deeply discounted. He probably ended up making two to three times the return of the custom- ers whose brokers sold them the Unit Trust. These unit trusts usually included one bond from Puerto Rico, which are greatly out of favor today because of the Islands financial problems. NC bonds were in demand at that time, and the bonds from the U S territories—which were also tax exempt for federal and state taxes—were stuck in the package. Another lesson: Why buy the packaged product when you can own the real thing, the bonds themselves?

Never buy a bond mutual fund, because the fees greatly re- duce your returns. If you are investing a large amount in mu- nicipal bonds, have your advisor contact the bond desk and have them custom build a portfolio to suit your needs, or deal directly with a municipal bond broker.

TOO GOOD TO BE TRUE

YEARS AGO I HEARD about a man who was planning on retiring with a 2 million dollar lump sum pension that he was going to invest with a company that promised him a 10 percent return for the rest of his life. I wonder if things worked out for him or if he ended up broke in his old age. Don't invest in things that are too good to be true. Selling things that are too good to be true is an old trick, but it still seems to work today.

FINANCIAL ADVICE ON THE INTERNET

THE INTERNET HAS A lot of useful information. Be careful and watch out for the companies that are trying to take advantage of investors.

RENTAL PROPERTY

RENTAL PROPERTY IS NOT for everyone. Those who manage their own properties do much better than those who use management companies. Avoid partnerships. If you can't afford the property yourself, don't buy it. The main reason that real estate has the ability to outperform the stock market is leverage. If you rent out properties that are paid for, you will not make any more over time than the market and you will have all of the headaches for nothing. Many people rent homes that they are unable to sell. This has the potential for disaster, especially if you have moved to another state.

The reason real estate can be very profitable is cash flow and leverage, which is also why real estate has the ability to lose lots of money. Not all real estate goes up in value. We seem to hear more about the successful people in real estate than the losers.

Uncle Tom used to say that "the reason the IRS allows deprecation was because it was a legitimate expense". The roof, heating and air, flooring, windows, paint, bathrooms, and appliances all wear out over time. Kitchens, bathrooms, flooring, and paint colors go out of style, reducing their value.

If you are going to get in the rental business, be careful not to borrow too much money and also be careful to protect yourself from a rise in interest rates. A rise in interest rates could greatly lower your return. Real estate and stocks lose value with a rise in interest rates as well. Daddy used the phrase "sticking your neck out" to describe the risk of borrowing money on investments.

DOCTOR AND THE COWS

DADDY USED TO TELL a story about a doctor who was riding with the rancher whom he had invested in cattle with. The rancher pointed to three cows that didn't look very healthy and said, "Those are three of your cows." This story could be any investment in which you are absentee. If you are an absentee investor, invest in stocks, bonds, REITs (never closed-in REITs where you get robbed), ETFs, low-cost mutual funds, and real estate that you understand. Buy real things that are worth what you pay for them minus a reasonable sales charge, and never pay an annual fee.

CHEATING ON TAXES

THE PROBLEM WITH CHEATING on taxes is when do you stop? If you cheat a little one year and get away with it, next year you are going to cheat more as your chances of getting caught increase. I was once asked when I sold real estate why I didn't get a little "paper bag money" instead of reporting the correct gain.(Paper bag money is a term used to describe an unreported cash transaction.) My answer was that if I started cheating on taxes, when do I stop? Also if I got caught taking a large amount in cash in an attempt to defraud the federal government, that would be enough for me to be put in prison, along with the person who paid me the cash. If I were put in prison, I wouldn't want to share a cell with someone who is there because of me.

Daddy had a client who went to federal court for income tax evasion, and he behaved like you were supposed to behave in court when you are guilty. He was not a nice man, but he acted polite for once in his life while in the courtroom. A little old lady on the jury" couldn't see sending that nice man to jail", and he got off without time.

The IRS is not stupid. They catch people every day. They know all of the tricks. The courts like to make examples out of tax cheats. The penalties can be severe. You owe the IRS for the rest of your life. Bankruptcy does not get you off the hook with the IRS.

Cheating on taxes is gambling.

CELL PHONE TOWER

I AM IN THE process of getting a cell phone tower on my timberland. I've been approached by investors who are willing to

COOPER PEEL « 25

buy my site, even before the tower was complete. They will put together a package of tower sites and sell them as limited partnerships to investors. I'm guessing that the limited partnership holders will settle for around two thirds of the value of the site. One trick used by the limited partnerships is to leverage the deal in order to advertize a higher rate of return in order to make the partnership more attractive.

If someone, or a group of investors, made their own deal with a tower owner they would be way ahead of the limited partnerships. They could also offer to buy a percentage from an owner. Why is it that people want to be sold on something instead of cutting out the middle man and doing things on their own.

PASSIVE INVESTING

PASSIVE INVESTING IS A proven way to make money. Passive investors make more money, have fewer headaches, and pay much less in taxes than those who try to beat the market. A small percentage of investors beat the indexes over time, but most don't. Much more money has been spent on trying to beat the market than has ever been made by the few that beat it. "The fallacy that many people buy into is that if it's so easy to get an average return with little or no work (through indexing), then just a little more work should yield a slightly higher return. The reality is that most people who try this end up doing much worse than average."[1] The financial services industry has always been against passive investing because it is not nearly as profitable for them as the active accounts. "The fees and commissions earned through active investing are considerably higher than what should be earned by telling the truth about passive investing and charging a fair fee for this advice."[2]

Benjamin Graham, Three Timeless Principals, Daniel Meyers, Investopedia, Feburary 23, 2009

Rick Ferri, Five Lies About Index Funds, Forbes, September 23, 2010

BONDS AND INTERST RATES

REMEMBER WHEN YOU WERE a kid on the seesaw and the kid that you were seesawing with would jump off when you were high, letting you fall quickly to the ground? That's what will happen to you, the bond investor, when interest rates rise. The longer the maturity, the worse the drop. There are some bond mutual funds that have a much higher rate of return than the bonds themselves. The reason that these funds have a higher rate of return is because they are leveraged. They have much more risk. These will really get hammered when interest rates go up. People invest in bonds because they want to avoid risk. I can't understand why anyone would want a leveraged bond fund? I know why the financial services industry makes them, in order to make them easier to sell so that the public doesn't buy the real thing, the bonds themselves, which they don't make as much money selling.. "If you must own government bonds, buy them outright from the Treasury and avoid the bond funds, in which you're paying management fees for nothing."[3]

I recently saw an article in *Barons,* where an adviser was charging a 1 percent fee not only on stocks but also on bonds. If your bonds were fifteen years to maturity, then the advisor would have charged you ten times what you should have paid if you bought the bonds outright. Buying bonds in a mutual fund greatly reduces your returns because of the fees. Fees eat up your returns in stock mutual funds as well, but with stocks they have more profit to play with. Always buy bonds or low cost ETFs instead of mutual funds. If safety is your goal, don't be tricked into yields that are too good to be true. At the present time, short to intermediate bond ETFs with low fees and no leverage gimmicks pay a little more than CDs. If you want to make more, then be prepared to take more risk.

Peter Lynch, Beating the Street, Simon and Schuster, New York, 1993, page 80

BUY AND HOLD ETF OR STOCK INSTEAD OF AN ANNUITY

YOU'VE PROBABLY SEEN SALES literature that mentions the *power of deferred income*. This is a slogan for a product that has minimal, and in most cases negative tax advantages, which I will explain in this chapter. A low-cost ETF will cost less for the rest of your life than the average variable annuity costs for one year.

Buy a low-cost ETF, instead of an annuity, and hold it for the long term. A really dumb idea that actually beats the annuity by leaps and bounds is to buy a low-cost S&P 500 ETF and throw away the dividend (around 2 percent at the present time). This will still beat the annuity that is invested in the S&P 500 because most annuities cost much more than the dividends. Most annuity owners don't believe that their annual fees or expenses cost as much as 3.5 percent a year. If you are dumb enough not to know how much you are paying, you deserve to be paying 3.5 percent a year. "Ninety per-cent of variable annuity contracts are still sold with income benefits that carry an average cost of 1 percent. Add that to the average 1.5 percent contract cost and 1 percent investment management fees, and investors are looking at annuity contracts costing upward of 3.5 percent." If you don't believe that you are paying that much in fees, look to see if you can find the dividends.

The ETF or the long-term buy-and-hold stock portfolio will smoke the annuity on tax savings. You have complete liquidity with stocks or ETFs, unlike the annuity, which has steep surrender charg-es and only allows a 10 percent distribution on the anniversary date. You don't have to wait until you are 59 1/2 to get to your money without a 10 percent IRS penalty. With the annuity, the taxes must be paid at some point, and then as ordinary income. With stocks or ETFs, the gains will be taxed as at the preferred long-term capital gains rate, if held for over a year. The dividends are taxed at the pre-ferred dividend rate. With the annuity if you are invested in stocks, you lose the tax break that the IRS allows to stock investors, which in most cases ends up costing an extra 13 percent (28 percent ordi-nary income minus 15 percent long term capital gains or dividends). With stocks and ETFs, the heirs receive a stepped-up basis: in other words, no income tax on the gain. With the annuity, the spouse can defer the gain, but it is still taxed as ordinary income. When received by heirs, all gains must be taxed as ordinary income in the year of death, which can be a huge tax disadvantage. Stocks or ETFs can be transferred as a gift to another individual, such as a grandchild, who could hold or sell them. This flexibility does not exist with the annu-ity. If you are receiving distributions from an annuity that invest in stocks, you could be in my Tax Inefficiency Chapter.

Barons, Top 50 Annuities, page 26, May 27, 2013

ANNUITY HOLE

IF YOU INVEST IN an annuity, years later when you have a considerable amount of taxable money in the annuity, you are in what I call the annuity hole. The financial advisor who gets to sell you a rollover annuity because you don't want to pay the taxes, is sitting in a good position to make a lot of money from you. Annuity hole is a good thing for the financial services industry and a bad thing for investors. You can avoid annuity hole by never buying an annuity. The only way to get out of annuity hole is to pay the taxes. Consider getting out of your annuity over a number of years, instead of all at once in order to reduce taxes.

LIFE INSURANCE

YOU BUY LIFE INSURANCE to protect against loss of income. Term insurance is much cheaper. When buying term life insurance, always make sure that you will be insured as long as the need for the insurance exists. If a 25 year old buys a 25 year level term policy, when that policy ends at age 50, he or she may not be able to get insurance, if in poor health. However, most term policies have a period of time where the insured has the option to convert to permanent life insurance with the same health rating as the initial policy. In shopping for term insurance, always consider the longer convertibility period. If a twenty-five year old buys a twenty-five year level term policy that was convertible to permanent life for the entire 25 years, then they would have an option at age 50 of permanent life insurance as opposed to little or no options if they were in bad health. Always know the date when you are no longer eligible to convert your term life policy. A few months prior to this date would be a good time to start shopping for a replacement policy. If you have serious health problems, you should consider taking advantage of the conversion.

Don't let an insurance salesperson do your thinking for you. If they start showing you how great life insurance is as an investment, then you should have them do their presentation in a conference with your accountant. All of the lies will go away in the accountants office. Paying an accountant for a one hour meeting with an insurance salesperson is money well spent.

Don't be insurance poor. There are life insurance salespeople who will try to show you that life insurance is a wonderful investment. They make over one and a half years annual premiums if you buy their policies. The performance history of the mutual insurance companies was supported by a robust stock, bond, and real estate market. The mutual insurance companies were heavily invested in the financial services industry which outperformed the market due to their ability to overcharge investors. The performance of the markets over the last thirty years was much better than the next thirty years will be. When you deal with a mutual insurance salesperson, keep in mind that, although you're not directly invested in the stock, bond, and real estate markets, your performance as a policy holder depends on those markets over time. There is no such thing as a free lunch: your returns must come from somewhere. Mutual insurance policies that are 30 years old have a rate of return of around 6 percent, 4 percent less than the market.

Variable life insurance is not a good deal for you. It is a wonderful deal for the financial services industry that charges over 3 percent a year on the variable accounts, plus the cost of the insurance. Life is too short for me to read a prospectus and the statement of additional expenses in order to find out the total annual expenses. Any investment in which it is difficult to determine the expenses will be overpriced. Please let me know if you find a packaged investment that isn't overpriced.

I hate to say this, but your financial future regarding life insurance is a result of the salesperson and the company you end up getting stuck with. There's a big difference between most financial advisors that will put you in low cost level term and the mutual insurance salesperson who will have you spend so much more for their whole life products. Avoid life insurance salespeople, but don't avoid taking care of your life insurance needs.

Always buy your insurance from an independent, not a captive agent. If you use a captive agent, don't assume that you are only paying a little more. With a captive agent, always request that they show you the competition's products as well as theirs. Compare prices if you suspect that the captive agent is not being honest. Ask them to explain why their product is worth the price difference. My first quote at my short-lived career as a captive agent was 150 percent more than my financial advisor could get on level term. The quote that I gave for level term was different in that it was always convertible to whole life, even though that was also overpriced. Captive agents are paid a higher percentage if they sell the company products. Many captive companies don't allow new agents to sell outside products. Captive agents only receive a retirement benefit on the sale of company products. Captive agents are taught that you, the customer, are buying them and that they are doing you a favor selling you insurance that costs 50 percent more.

Always buy insurance on your own when required for a loan, or replace it as soon as possible in order to save a bundle of money over time.

Riders are never as competitive as the policy itself. It's like when you buy china, a place setting is much more affordable than the add-ons, like the teapot or creamer. One rider that is completely stupid is accidental death, where your beneficiaries receive double if you die in an accident. This is stupid mainly because dying of natural causes is in most cases much more of a financial burden on your family. Instead of this rider, use the extra money to buy more real insurance to protect your family. If the insurance companies offered a natural causes rider that would pay double if you died of natural causes, then this would be worth looking at. They don't because the odds are against them. The insurance companies are not stupid, and you should not be either.

WHOLE LIFE OR BUY TERM AND INVEST THE DIFFERENCE

LESS THAN 2 PERCENT of term life policies pay death claims. This figure is misleading since most people who have term life insurance have several policies during their lifetime. I've had three. One of the dumbest lines that insurance agents have used over the years is *you are throwing money away by buying term life insurance.* Nothing could be further from the truth.

Another lie is that insurance is cheaper or a better deal when you are young. Insurance is cheaper when you are young because of the time value of money, which you or your salesperson may not understand, but the insurance company does. If you buy the same policy years later at the same health rating, you will find the same insurance cost table in it. You should buy insurance when you are young in order to make smaller payments, to take advantage of your health, and to take advantage of the time value of money.

If a person had not made the mistakes of many investors for the past thirty years, they would have much more money if they had bought term and invested the difference. If they bought a low-cost S&P 500 or broad-based ETF and reinvested the dividends, they would be way ahead. If your investments performed like many investors, who because of high expenses in mutual funds or managed money, unnecessary taxes due to high turnover, excessive trading, and emotions that tend to make people sell during market lows and buy during market highs, then whole life with one of the mutual companies could be worth more money today. Another argument for life insurance as an investment is that it disciplines the investor to make payments. I've never known of anyone dumping an insurance policy during a correction. The reason that some of the mutual companies have performed so well is because they are invested in stocks, bonds, and real estate.

AVOID THE LIFE INSURANCE SALESPERSON

IT'S ALRIGHT TO AVOID life insurance salespeople if you are certain that your life insurance needs are taken care of. Don't be someone who successfully avoided life insurance salespeople and died without adequate life insurance , or was unable to get much needed life insurance due to bad health when older because of poor planning, or lack of planning.

GROUP LIFE INSURANCE

BUYING GROUP LIFE INSURANCE instead of a personal policy is a mistake. Many people buy group life insurance because they think that being a benefit, it must be a good deal. Another reason, which is understandable, is to avoid life insurance salespeople. If you are in good health, you can get a level term life policy on your own that will better serve your needs. If you have your own term life policy and end up in bad health, you can convert it to permanent insurance, if you are in the convertibility period, at the same health rating as when the policy was purchased. With group life you can convert if you are no longer employed by the company, to a very expensive permanent policy. Converting a group life insurance policy is expensive because only people who are in bad health take this option.

HOW MUCH LIFE INSURANCE DO I NEED?

WHEN CALCULATING HOW MUCH life insurance you need, consider everything. Take all of your debts and obligations, investment income, retirement, and Social Security. Assume your investments will make a modest rate of return. The market might do 7 percent over time, but 4 percent would be a much safer projection of how your money will perform, especially if you are paying 2 percent on mutual funds. Buy more life insurance than you need, and make sure you are covered until the need for the insurance ends. If you have a medical condition where life insurance isn't affordable, you need to change your financial plan.

NOBODY EVER LOST MONEY WITH LIFE INSURANCE

THIS IS NOT A true statement. The states have a pool of money in case an insurance company goes bankrupt. Carriers operating in a state may be required to contribute more in the event of a bankruptcy. A bankrupt insurance company can be very difficult for a state insurance pool to handle. Insurance companies that have been rescued freeze withdrawals for many years in order to make them more lucrative to the insurance company taking over the policies. If you die, you get your money. If you want to borrow or take a distribution, you may be forced to pay a severe penalty, thus lose money. The Baldwin United policies from the 1980's had withdrawal penalties over 10 percent. Nobody has lost money if they didn't need their money, or died, during the time that the policies were frozen. The honest answer is that people have lost money with life insurance.

RESORT PROPERTY

DADDY SAID, "DON'T MIX up your vacation with your investments. If you can afford to go to the beach, then you can afford to rent." Resort property is not a good investment. It is not well utilized. The insurance, taxes, utilities, and maintenance fees are high. You are always absent, so you need to pay others to do things that you would normally do on your own, such as change a light bulb, which can cost $15. Having property in a location far away can be more stressful and expensive than owning local properties. Avoid real estate salespeople that prey upon vacationers with promises of high investment returns. Many people buy resort property to satisfy their ego, a proven way to lose money. Consider owning your own office instead of resort property. Put the ass of your car to the cottage or ski chalet when leaving your vacation.

HOME AND AUTO INSURANCE

I FIND IT DIFFICULT to understand why so many people don't shop their insurance. If you are not with an independent agent, then at least shop your insurance to see how much more you are paying with your captive agent. If you add up your insurance cost, you will find it to be one of your largest expenses. Many insurance company software programs will present a policy with a $250 deductible.. A good agent will always show you the higher deductibles as a way to save you money. If they don't, get a better agent, one that cares about you, the customer. Always go for the higher deductable if you can save the deductable amount in a reasonable number of years. Keep in mind that claims are not free. The insurance companies share your claims history. Claims are a bad thing to have, and they stay with you for the rest of your life. I am sure there's some bean counter at the insurance company who is smart enough to know the dollar amount at which you would be better off paying the claim yourself instead of having another claim added to your claims history. I'm not that smart, but I figure that I'm better off paying any claim, other than medical, under $1,000 out of pocket. In some states auto claims under a certain amount or necessary equipment such as headlights and taillights don't hurt your claims history. Ask your agent. Higher deductibles will save you a wad of money over time. You would also file fewer claims with the higher deductable. Use the insurance for what it is meant: to cover an expense that would be difficult or impossible for you to handle on your own.

Insurance companies on average pay back half of what is paid in. Insurance is not a good investment, but it is necessary. Use insurance to insure the events that you cannot cover yourself and you will save a lot money.

UMBRELLA

SAVE MONEY BY SHOPPING your insurance and having higher deductibles. Don't save money on insurance by not being able to cover a catastrophic event. An example would be if you were responsible for a multi car wreck in which several people were injured. The best auto insurance policy could reach its limit quickly. Even if you don't have any net worth to protect, get the umbrella to protect those who might be injured by you or your family. It is the right thing to do.

HOW GREAT ARE THE BROKERAGE FIRMS?

REMEMBER HOW MANY BROKERAGE firms we lost due to the mortgage crisis? Remember how many of the highly paid people that were handling our mutual funds in the World Trade Center who weren't smart enough to have any life insurance at all? Our tax money bailed out their families. I remember when all of my mutual funds were heavily invested in Enron. Look at how many people in the financial services industry that sell annuities because of tax savings that just aren't there. I've never known anyone who was told to invest in Berkshire Hathaway by their advisors. The industry doesn't use the word kickback, but many mutual fund companies give incentives to brokers who sell large amounts of their funds. Don't be fooled by all of the advertising. The industry is not that great at making you money or helping you save on taxes. It never was. The financial services industry is great at making lots of money from investors. Uncle Tom used to say that "If you listen to stock brokers, you'll sleep in the streets".

"Most advisors, however, are far better at generating high fees than they are at generating high returns. In truth, their core competence is salesmanship.."

Warren Buffett, Berkshire Hathaway 2014 Annual Report, page 19

IS HAVING AN ASSET MODEL WORTH 1 PERCENT A YEAR?

NO.

People are starting to wise up about how much money the mutual fund industry has been costing them lately, so the financial services industry has had to come up with new ways to soak investors. It didn't take them long to come up with charging for asset allocation or managed ETFs.

TAX INEFFICIENCY

THIS IS THE ONLY financial book that has a chapter on how to do things the wrong way.

There is only one way an annuity can be tax efficient. If you defer ordinary income in a cash annuity until a later date and then take the gain at the same or lower tax bracket, then you will have saved the income produced by the deferral. If you did this with a variable annuity, you will have taken an investment subject to dividend and capital gains treatment (lower taxes) and turned it into ordinary income (higher taxes). You have deferred income in order to pay more taxes than if you had invested in real estate, stocks, ETFs, or mutual funds. If you need to take 10,000 dollars out of an annuity or stock that you have held long enough to have doubled your investment, your taxes on the annuity will be 3,480 dollars (assuming 28% federal and 6.8% state on every dollar taken out since all gains are taxable until you get to the basis, which is not taxed) and 1,090 dollars on the stock (assuming 15% capital gains for the federal and 6.8% state on the 5,000 dollars that was the taxable gain, the other 5,000 dollars being your basis, which is not taxable).

Mutual funds have a basis that, on established funds is much lower than what you paid for the fund. Every year mutual funds report capital gains that are taxable to you even if you don't have a profit in the fund. This is the only way that I know of where you pay taxes on someone else's capital gains.

Everyone is pushing 529 plans to help fund future college expenses. You never hear much about Uniform Gift to Minor accounts, where appreciated assets can be transferred to the children. A very tax-inefficient move would be to sell stock in order to fund a 529 plan instead of placing the stock in the child's name and then selling it now or at a later date. The industry does not talk much about Uniform Gift to Minor accounts because it is a buy and hold strategy that doesn't pay sales charges or annual fees.

The winner at tax inefficiency is when a customer gets talked into selling a long-term stock position all at once in order to invest the money in mutual funds or managed money in order to be diversified. No consideration is given to the customer to sell the stock slowly over time in order to reduce taxes. If the sale was large enough to trigger the alternative minimum tax (AMT), the federal tax rate would go from the long term capital gains rate of 15 percent to the AMT rate of 28 percent. If the customer had a 90 percent profit on their stock, they would owe 28 percent AMT plus 6.8 percent (average state income tax rate). The customer would have 68.8 percent of their original investment after taxes It will take one hell of a long time for the remaining 68.8 percent with fees of 2 percent imposed by the financial services industry—plus the additional taxes from account turnover—to catch up to the stock that didn't have any annual fees or expenses at all. The financial services industry really made a monkey out of this investor. Bad advice is timeless, always costing the customer more in taxes. In this situation, which has happened many times, the customer paid heavily to be diversified. The financial services industry will tell you that buy and hold is not the way to make money, but they don't have any problem selling you out of your profitable buy and hold positions in order to make them money. Often the advisor will not charge a commission on a large position that they stand to make a lot of money from. Don't consider this a favor. The efficient way would be to manage an existing portfolio by selling stocks slowly over time in order to reduce the tax bite, and then investing in low cost ETFs. When taking a large capital gain, always check with your accountant first to see how much you can save by selling stock slowly over time, or not at all. Ask them if they agree with my advice.

If you have not considered converting your retirement into a Roth, you may be missing out on one of the best tax savings opportunities out there.

Deferring income is not always good planning. The taxes must be paid at some point, unless used to cover medical expenses or given to charity. Annuities, unless inherited by a spouse, must be liquidated in the year of death, which can be a huge tax disadvantage. IRAs or 401Ks can be spread out over a number of years depending on whether the owner was taking required distributions or not. Years ago when federal income and estate taxes were higher, it was possible for an IRA to have a negative value after taxes. The owner in the highest estate tax bracket, who lived in the state with the highest inheritance and income taxes, and was in the highest federal income tax bracket could owe more in taxes than the IRA was worth. That could not happen today, but it still is a good example of the reduced value of monies that have taxes due. Timberland, or Berkshire Hathaway stock, since it doesn't pay a dividend, is the best way that I know to defer income outside of retirement plans. If you are young and in the 15 percent federal income tax bracket, you should not put 15 percent in your 401K, but put at least 12 percent in your Roth 401K or Roth IRA instead.

Not listing your dependents as contingent beneficiaries on retirement accounts can be a tax disadvantage in that they will be required to liquidate the accounts with a much faster timetable if they inherit the accounts without being listed. They also would be subject to probate if not listed as beneficiaries.

MANAGED ETFS

SOME BROKERAGE FIRMS HAVE started charging an annual fee to invest in ETFs that they" manage" for you. Buy broad based low-cost ETFs and hold them for the long term, without annual fees. How difficult is it to pick out a low-cost broad based index ETF and hold it for the long term? The buy and hold strategy that I recommend will not only save you a lot of money in fees and expenses, but will also save you on taxes. If a financial advisor tries to talk you out of buy and hold, then you are better off without them. No advice is better than bad advice.

WHY CAN'T THE FINANCIAL SERVICES INDUSTRY CHARGE BY THE HOUR LIKE LAWYERS AND ACCOUNTANTS?

THE IDEA OF GETTING free advice from someone who is peddling overpriced products is ludicrous.

We would get better financial advice from an advisor who wasn't being paid from selling products. Some advisors are paid on a fee-only basis costing 1 percent or more annually based on assets under management. That's more than lawyers and accountants make by the hour. The way that the financial services industry is set up has too much overhead for advisors to charge the same hourly rates as lawyers and accountants. Lawyers and accountants have much more education than financial advisors. They are held accountable. They don't make you sign an arbitration agreement. I know people who lost money due to being sold bad financial products that ended up with little or no settlement.

Use the interest-rate calculator on the Internet to see for your-self how much 1to 2 percent will cost you over time. One percent of a 7 percent return, which is a reasonable expectation for the market to perform in the future, is 14 percent of your profit. Two percent of a 7 percent rate of return is 28 percent of your profit. Overpaying for financial services is not the way to financial success.

A few advisors are starting to charge by the hour, which is the way that you deserve to be treated.

I WILL MANAGE YOUR 401K FOR 1/2 PERCENT

I RECEIVED A LETTER recently from an advisor who wanted to help me manage my 401K for 1/2% percent a year. She insulted my intel-ligence when she implied that one of the benefits would be to help me save on my expenses. In order to save on my expenses, all I need to do is invest in individual stocks if offered, or the broadest base ETF in the plan. Your 401K is already costly enough without adding 1/2% percent more a year in unnecessary fees and expenses. The total of 1/2% percent of a 7 percent rate of return is 7 percent of your profit. If you take the time to study it, you will find your 401K to be costing way more in fees and expenses than you thought.

SURRENDER CHARGES

IF YOU ARE SOLD an investment that you want out of that has steep surrender charges, compare the cost of the fees and expenses to the surrender charges. How much does it cost to get out verses how verses much does it cost to stay in? You will find that the fees and expenses which are usually difficult to determine are close to the surrender charges, and you'll be penalized whether you stay in or get out. You could try to get out without a penalty if you weren't honestly shown the fees and expenses by your advisor. Good luck. Take your losses and learn from your mistakes if you want out.

Never buy a product that has surrender charges. Always invest things that are real, that are worth what you pay for them minus a reasonable sales charge. Never buy anything packaged, or pay annual fees and expenses.

OLD NATIONAL GEOGRAPHICS

YOU'RE WONDERING WHAT THIS has to do with investing. If you had invested in all of the companies that were successful enough to have one-page ads in National Geographic thirty years ago, you would not have done very well. You would have done poorly with the airlines, car manufactures, camera, and film companies. The oil companies, however, might have make up for your losses. The point here is that when we pick individual stocks, we tend to pick winners. Our emotions don't make us money. Yesterday's winners can turn into tomorrow's losers. This is another reason why most people should buy ETFs, low cost mutual funds, or Berkshire Hathaway.

INVESTMENTS THAT IMPLY THAT YOU CAN ALWAYS GET YOUR MONEY BACK

SOME INVESTMENTS ARE SOLD with the implication that the right of first refusal by the managing partner means that they will buy you out, at your cost, in the future, if requested. Nothing could be further from the truth. What are they going to buy you out with? Only invest in things that are worth what you pay for them, minus a reasonable sales charge. Never buy too good to be true investments that are neatly packaged, especially the ones that don't honestly disclose sales charges. The prospectus discloses the charges and expenses if you are smart enough, or dumb enough, to fish through it, but why. Life is too short to study investments that are designed to overcharge you. These investments are just a continuation of the old limited partnerships from days past. Ask any older investor how well they turned out. If Limited Partnerships had turned out well the financial services industry would still be selling them using the same name.

INVESTMENTS THAT IMPLY THAT YOU CAN'T LOSE MONEY

I SEE A LOT of investments being sold on TV or the internet that imply that they are safer than the stock market with almost the same rate of return. They imply that you can't lose money. Things that are too good to be true, aren't. It's that simple.

SEMINARS WITH FREE DINNERS

STAY HOME. BUY YOUR own dinner. All of these seminars imply that they are going to teach you something outstanding, like how to get more from Social Security, or more income in retirement, or helping you plan for long term care needs, but in truth all they are doing is trying to get their hands on your investments in order to make 2 percent a year from you, or to sell you an expensive long term care policy. The dinner is the bait, and you are the fish.

WALK AWAY AT THE FIRST HINT OF DISHONESTY

IF YOU SEE ANYTHING that doesn't seem honest about an advisor or a financial services company, don't deal with them. Every time that I have had dealings with a person that I knew was dishonest, I have regretted it. There are a lot of dishonest financial advisors out there.

CLOSED-IN REITS

CLOSED IN REITS ARE designed to take advantage of investors. The day you buy them, they are worth around eighty-five cents on the dollar. In order to make them easier to sell, they are officially worth what you pay for them until the offering is sold out. The reason that there is no secondary market for Closed end REITs is to keep investors in the dark as to their value. Investing in things that are worth only 85 cents on the dollar is no way to money. If you would like to know the value, find the book value from the annual report. As with all packaged investments, they do not disclose a sales charge. I have never seen a packaged investment that wasn't overpriced. Invest in things that are real, that are worth what you pay for them, minus a reasonable sales charge.

If you own Closed-In-REITs, you have no choice but to hold on to them until maturity. Before maturity, you will get a letter from a group of investors who are offering to buy out shareholders. Look up the most recent book value from the annual report, and their offer will be around 20 cents on the dollar.

SIMPLICITY

ONE KEY TO DEVELOPING a strategy to win a war or a ball game is simplicity. Plans that are too complicated have a greater chance of failure. The same is true with your investments.

LUNCH FOR IDIOTS

IF YOU ARE BEING taken out to lunch four times a year by your advisor, you are paying too much. Ask them to lower their fees, and use that money to buy your own lunch. Better yet, try a buy and hold strategy and take a vacation four times a year, instead of lunch with your savings.

LIQUIDITY

LIQUIDITY IS A GOOD thing. Packaged products offered by the financial services industry reduce liquidity.

VARIBLE LIFE INSURANCE

DON'T EVEN THINK ABOUT buying a variable life insurance policy until you read through the prospectus and the statement of additional information well enough to figure out what it really costs. Most variable life insurance policies charge over 3 percent in annual fees and expenses on funds held within the account, plus the cost of the insurance. If an advisor gives you the total cost of a mutual fund, annuity, or variable life insurance without taking several hours to figure it out, they are wrong. If they tell you the published annual expenses, they are only not telling you the total cost. Not many people would buy them if they were told the truth about the cost. If the S&P 500 has an annual return of 7 percent, then you will have an annual return of only 4 percent, minus the cost of your insurance. Why not invest your money in a low-cost ETF and pocket the 3 percent, and buy your own term insurance with the savings. Most advisors don't understand the policies well enough to know the fees and expenses, but they all know how much they make selling them.

FIFTY-SECOND BIRTHDAY

WHEN YOU TURN FIFTY-TWO, ask yourself whether you would have been better off if you had worked in a state job for thirty years and were able to take full retirement. Government retirement plans are much better than private industry. They are especially attractive to those who start young.

Ask yourself how well your investments performed in relation to the S&P 500. If you invested 10,000 dollars in Vanguards S&P 500 index in 1976, it would be worth over 514,000 dollars in 2014. Most investors do not do nearly as well as the S&P 500. If your investments managed to keep up with S&P 500, was your portfolio as tax efficient ? If you have been in mutual funds for a long time, consider how much you have paid in fees, expenses, and taxes.

THE MAN ABOVE MARILYN MONROE

I READ AN ARTICLE about a gentleman who spent over two million dollars to be buried in the mausoleum above Marilyn Monroe. Later, his heirs sold the burial site for over four million dollars and moved him somewhere else, much cheaper of course. The second owner had an attorney make sure that his kids weren't able to sell his spot. All of the children had to agree to sell the burial site and move the body, and the motivation was money. I'm sure that the IRS wanted income and estate tax on the burial site, since it would not be listed as an asset in his estate. This is an example of how badly children can behave after their parents are gone.

BOX OF ROCKS

PAPPY USED TO TELL a story about an old man who gave all of his material possessions to his children. They were to take turns keeping him in their homes. This worked out well at first, but after a while, the families were not very excited when it was their turn to take care of him. One day a metal lock box showed up, which he always kept in his possession. He carried it with him everywhere he went. It got heaver over time. He started getting treated better. The second that He died, all of the family rushed over to the box and broke off the lock. They found a box full of rocks with a note that said, "Don't leave everything to your children until you are dead."

SELLING SOMETHING THAT YOU DON'T KNOW THE VALUE OF

THIS SOUNDS TOO DUMB to put in a book, but it happens often. People actually sell real estate or timber without taking the time to determine its value. This happens more often with inherited property. There are people who make a living buying property cheap from others. Always tell your children the value and plans that you might have for real estate that they might own one day. My mother warned me about a farmer who owned land adjacent to ours, and not to consider his low ball offer if she died.

IOUS AND COSIGHNED LOANS

IF THERE EVER WAS a timeless bad investment, the IOU to family, in-laws, and friends wins the prize. Not only will you lose money, but you will be hated for trying to collect. A good way to avoid getting stuck with a bad loan from family and friends is to require references from people that they have made unsecured loans to, which were paid back on time. A worse mistake than loaning money is to cosign a loan. Over 80 percent of cosigned loans end up in trouble, which means that the cosigner ends up in trouble.

Years ago a worker in my hometown went to his boss with papers for a loan. He said: "Mr. Clayton at the bank said that if you sign these papers, that he will loan me some money". The boss said:" tell Mr. Clayton that if he signs the papers, that I will loan you the money".

SET UP YOUR ESTATE TO AVOID PROBATE

YOUR LIFE INSURANCE, ANNUITIES, and retirement accounts go to your heirs without probate. Probate, or the process of an estate going through the court system, can be very costly. Always list your children as contingent beneficiaries in order to avoid probate. Real estate and bank accounts can also be set up to avoid probate. Avoiding probate will save your heirs a considerable amount of time, money, and legal fees.

PATIENCE

AN INVESTOR NEEDS PATIENCE to be successful. If you are low on patience like myself, make an effort to have more.

KNOWING WHEN TO TAKE A LOSS

NOT ALL INVESTMENTS MAKE money. Sometimes it is necessary to take a loss. Don't be too proud to take a loss.

CHASING WINNERS

INVESTING IN MUTUAL FUNDS or money managers because they have outperformed the market is a proven way to achieve inferior investment results. " This is another national pastime, reviewing the past performance of funds. Thousands of hours are devoted to it. Books and articles are written about it. Yet with few exceptions, this turns out to be a waste of time. "

Investing in companies or sectors that have underperformed the market has proven to be a much more successful approach than chasing winners.

Peter Lynch, Beating The Street, Simon and Schuster, New York,1993, page 68

TAX EFFICIENT

BUY AND HOLD CORE stocks, or low cost broad based ETFs. You will have no annual fees unless you buy or sell, except for the ETFs, which are minimal. Your dividends will be taxed at the preferred dividend rate. If you sell after a year, you will be taxed at the preferred long-term capital gains rate. If you never sell, your heirs will receive your stocks with a stepped-up basis(they can sell them without any tax). The question is will the mutual funds or money managers beat the market by enough to cover their fees and expenses, plus the additional tax incurred by a portfolio that trades more often? The answer is no, in most cases they don't. Over 75 percent of stock mutual funds and money managers lag the S&P 500 over time.

INVEST IN COMPANIES THAT MAKE THINGS PEOPLE MUST HAVE

UNCLE TOM USED TO say, "Invest in companies that make things that people must have.

"Make your own mutual fund by buying quality stocks that pay good dividends and hold them for the long term." Consider core stocks (stocks that are leaders in their industries). Core stocks hold up better when times are bad and do well when times are good. Only invest in companies that you understand. Don't invest in stocks if you think that you might panic and sell during a correction. Corrections are the time to buy, not sell. Always check your stocks at least quarterly. Value Line, which is at your library, is an excellent way to keep up with your stocks. Do not have too many stocks to keep up with or too few not to be diversified.

THINGS THAT ADVISORS WON'T TELL YOU

1. Buy Berkshire Hathaway and hold it for the long term.
2. Buy and hold quality stocks that pay good dividends and hold them for the long term.
3. Buy and hold low-cost ETFs and hold them for the long term.
4. That their products or services will probably not make you as much money after taxes over time as the investments listed above.

THE WAY THINGS USED TO BE

IN THE OLD DAYS, stockbrokers sold mostly individual stocks and bonds for a one-time commission. It was hard work picking stocks. They didn't sell as many mutual funds, which they could blame losses on. Mutual funds fees and expenses were reasonable in the old days. They didn't have low-cost ETFs until 1974. They did not dare ask the customers for 1 percent or more a year to manage their money. People back then were not that dumb.

TIME-SHARE

BUYING A TIMESHARE IS one of the dumbest financial mistakes that you could ever make. I don't call it an investment. A good rule of thumb is to never invest with girls that approach you on the beach in bikinis. Many time-shares are only worth thirty cents on the dollar on the secondary market the day you buy them. None of them can be sold without losing money. To make matters worse, the IRS will not let you write off a loss from a time share because they don't consider it to be real estate. If you are told that you can get your money back at some later date, ask from whom? There is no pot of gold to pay you with. They are giving you a guarantee with no resources to back it up. A lottery ticket, which in most states is worth around fifty-five cents on the dollar, is worth more than many time-shares. The old saying *cash is king,* makes for a much better vacation plan. Put the ass of your car to your vacation rental at the end of your vacation, and invest your money elsewhere.

CAPITAL GAINS RATE

TAKE A LARGE CAPITAL gain without checking with your accountant and you might get a surprise at tax season. A large capital gain can put you in AMT which is a 28 percent tax rate. In other words, the 15 percent capital gains rate may not apply to you if you take a large capital gain.

THE BEST REAL ESTATE INVESTMENT:YOUR OFFICE

A FRIEND JUST RENTED his building to a group of doctors. I told him that at least one of them had a beach cottage as an investment, while they rented his office. If you're going to be in an office for your career, you are going to pay for it. Why not own it? You are renting to yourself, with no middleman. You can do your own small repairs. Don't ever consider buying vacation property, a poor investment, before owning your own office, a good investment.

SHARED VACATION HOMES

UNCLE TOM USED TO say, "The nearest thing to nothing, was owning a beach cottage with someone else."

WHAT PERCENT SHOULD I INVEST IN STOCKS?

THERE IS AN OLD rule of thumb that you should be invested your age minus 120 in stocks. Why not have the percentage of your investments that should be invested in stocks based on your ability to handle risk, not your age? Consider core stocks that have a history of increasing dividends, a broad-based ETF, or Berkshire Hathaway if you are looking for safety. Over time, stocks and real estate have always beat fixed investments. Another advantage of stocks is that dividends are taxed at a lower rate than fixed investments,13 percent lower if you are in the 28 percent tax bracket.

Young people should be fully invested. If you can afford to ride the ups and downs in the market, then you can afford to be fully invested. If you have low debt, then you have more ability to be fully invested. Older people should consider less-volatile investments if they cannot handle the down cycles of the markets. If you have a need for money from your investments in the next few years, use fixed investments to cover the need.

LEVERAGE

LEVERAGE IS A PROVEN way to make money and also a proven way to lose money. When you leverage your investments, you lower the safety of them.

I had a friend who was invested in a REIT that invested in pine timberland that was making more in dividends than I was making with my timberland that I owned outright. I couldn't understand why the real thing, timberland, wasn't as profitable as a REIT that owned timberland. I finally figured out that they were achieving the rate of return through leverage. Many packaged products use leverage to prop up their returns, making them more attractive to the uninformed investor, in order to make them easier to sell. Don't be fooled, packaged investments are made for the seller, not the buyer. Only invest in real investments that are worth what you pay for them minus a reasonable sales charge, without unnecessary expenses.

DISABILITY PLAN

EVERYONE HAS A DISABILITY plan. If you don't have disability insurance and you need your income, then your plan is to lose everything that you have, with the exception of Social Security benefits for disability. You have a much greater chance of being disabled during your working years than dying. The most affordable plans are those offered by an employer. If you are self-employed, disability insurance is expensive. Don't use the excuse that you can't afford disability insurance. Get $1,000 per month disability coverage instead of nothing. At least you will have a plan, which you can increase later.

GOLD

WHY BUY THE METAL when you can own the stock? Precious-metal stocks can be more volatile than the metal itself, but as a long-term investment, offer more. Mining companies are making money and growing, which is better than buying metal and having to pay to store it. I consider investing in precious-metal stocks or ETFs to be a gamble for the short-term investor. Newmont Mining has paid a dividend since 1934. An ounce of gold purchased in 1934 is still an ounce of gold with no return. One highly aggressive investment is leveraged

ETFs that own precious metal stocks. These are made for the real gamblers.

LOTTERY

I ASKED A MAN who had a large quantity of lottery tickets to cash in at a convenience store if he knew what percentage the state paid out on the lottery. He looked at me like I was an idiot.

It is disgraceful that our states have gotten themselves into a financial situation where they must have a lottery. Years ago, I told a man that I invested in the stock market instead of lottery tickets that only pay back fifty-five cents on the dollar. He told me that he could never invest in the stock market because he might lose money. The lottery is a tax on the poor and stupid. People who play the lottery tend to do it often. Ask educated people how much the power ball jackpot is and most don't know. Ask the uneducated and poor if you want to know the amount of the jackpot. Most lottery players lose a large amount of money over time. It is a terrible habit, one that you do not want your children to pick up. Notice how much the younger generation likes to play the lottery. I recommend that anyone who spends over $100 a year on the lottery keep a journal. If you keep a journal long enough, you will see that the lottery, or any other form of gambling, is a losers game, unless you are the house.

Whenever you get talked into loaning money to family, in-laws, or friends, chances are they are lottery players. Mention to them that they could have avoided the lottery and saved some of the money that you have just turned into an IOU. Require that they sign an agreement stating that they will not play the lottery until your loan is paid back.

OTHER PEOPLES MONEY

IF YOU SEE A commercial property being built in a location where you wonder who would take such a risk, the answer is simple: the property is being built with other people's money. The developers who talk others into investing in property make money, while many times the investors lose money. This is another example of the doctor and the cows.

EXCESS MONEY IN LIFE INSURANCE POLICY

IF YOU HAVE A permanent life insurance policy and develop health problems with a short life expectancy when you are middle age, this may save a lot of money. Life insurance policies are designed to be funded in order to make it to your life expectancy. If you are middle age, the policies may have excess money in them. Be extremely careful when doing this. Stop paying on the policy, thus burning up the excess money in order to pay for your insurance. This is the only way for you to get to the excess money. If you borrow from the excess money, they take it off your death benefit. If you die, the insurance company keeps all excess money in the account. Always check with your insurance company to make sure that you don't lose coverage. My family saved an annual premium because I figured this out before my mother passed. If we had been fat, dumb, and happy like most people, the insurance company would have pocketed another annual premium.

TAKE LOSS TO COVER WINDFALL

IF YOU HAVE A windfall, look for things that you can take a loss on to help reduce your taxes. If you have a stock, bond, mutual fund, or ETF with a loss that you would like to hold until it recovers, consider selling and replacing it with a similar stock, bond, mutual fund, or ETF. You cannot buy your initial security back for thirty-one days or you will trigger the IRS wash rule, thus nullifying your loss. With mutual funds, many times you can switch to a similar fund in the same family with no charges. Don't sell your mutual fund outright in order not to lose your initial sales charge.

EXCHANGE FUNDS

ANOTHER OPTION FOR AN investor who has too much of one stock is to roll the stock into an exchange fund. This is where brokerage firms accept stock from different companies and build a Unit Trust that allows the investor to put their shares without it being a taxable event. At the end of the holding period, the investor gets a diversified unit trust. The exchange fund only takes a certain amount of stocks from different companies when they build an issue. This might be smarter than paying capital gains or AMT if you need to diversify. When dealing with the financial services industry, always know the cost of an investment. Many times, the company offering the unit trust keeps the dividends as an annual expense. They are charging too much if they do this.

If several stockholders got together and wanted to make their own exchange fund, they would have to set up an LLC and use the IRS 721 Exeter Exchange.

BOND SWAP

AT SOME POINT IN the near future, interest rates are going to rise, causing losses on bonds and bond mutual funds. A smart tax strategy would be to sell the bonds or mutual funds at a loss and buy a similar bond or mutual fund. You cannot repurchase your original position for thirty-one days, or it will trigger the IRS wash rule, thus nullifying your loss. With the mutual fund, pick another mutual fund in the same family in order not to lose the sales charges. Your loss can be used to offset gains now or in the future. You can write off $3,000 a year against ordinary income and carry over the rest. This strategy is called a bond swap. It can also be done with stocks.

COLLEGE SAVINGS

529 PLANS ARE THE most popular option for college savings today. All monies from the 529 plan can be used tax free to cover education expenses. You can use a 529 plan from any state. Some states require that you participate in their plan in order to get tax free status. Most 529 plans are too conservative for many investors, not being fully invested in stocks in the early years, and reducing the stock exposure as the child gets closer to college age. The expenses are much higher than buy and hold stocks or ETFs.

Your Roth IRA can be used as a college savings tool. You can withdraw your principal after five years without being taxed and leave the rest in the account for your retirement. The Roth IRA has tax advantages for your heirs as well. They can inherit the Roth IRA and continue the tax free status based on their life expectancy. My children could still be receiving tax free distributions over 80 years after I opened my Roth IRA, making it by far the best tax savings option available. You have full control of the investments and expenses in a Roth IRA. You could save a considerable amount of money on fees and expenses with a Roth IRA with a low cost, buy and hold strategy. You have the ability to be a more aggressive investor than the 529 plans, which are one size fits all. Your Roth or any retirement plan does not have to be listed as an asset when applying for financial aid.

You can withdraw funds from your IRA or 401K without a penalty to cover certain college expenses.

Uniform Gift to Minor accounts are the place to put gifts of stock. Never sell stock in order to fund a 529 plan. Why sell stock at your tax rate when you can sell it at the child's tax rate, or sell it later? Sell the stock in the child's name and the first $1,000 will not be taxed. The second $1,000 will be taxed at the child's tax rate, and after that the account is taxed at the parents rate. The custodian has control until age eighteen or twenty-one, depending on the state. After that, the account becomes the child's, whether they go to college or not. A Uniform Gift to Minor account would have to be listed as an asset when applying for financial aid.

A few states have prepaid tuition programs where you are able to lock in current tuition rates.

A Clifford Trust is where you can keep an asset but transfer the income to someone else who will be taxed instead of you. It could be used to reduce taxes. This must be for a period of not less than ten years, and must be set up by an attorney.

Permanent life insurance can also be used to fund college. You can borrow against the cash value. Life insurance is not a good investment, but compared to CDs lately, it looks better.

BUY AND DON'T BE SOLD

DON'T SIGN ON THE dotted line until you have time to think over what you are doing. Just say no. The markets won't wait for you, but all of the overpriced packaged investments and insurance products will. Look at the surrender charges, which are clearly presented to you. If they are high, then you can believe the fees and expenses are high also, even if they are well hidden in the prospectus. Life is too short to figure out hidden fees and expenses. A good way to stay out of trouble is to never buy an investment with surrender charges. An even better way to stay out of trouble is to never buy any packaged investments. The reason that investments are packaged is to overcharge investors. I recommend buying the real thing: stocks, bonds, REITs (and never closed-in REITs, which is just a way of robbing you), ETFs, and low-cost mutual funds. Pay an honest advisor a full-service commission if you feel that you don't want to do things on your own, or even better find an advisor that charges by the hour. Don't be talked into paying an annual percentage of your assets to financial advisors unless your goal is to be much poorer in your old age. Don't be fooled into believing that they will make you so much more over time that their fees won't eat into your returns. All of my investments are worth what I pay for them, minus a reasonable commission or sales charge, without an annual fee.

ASK OLD INVESTORS ABOUT THEIR LIMITED PARTNERSHIP EXPERENCES

THE PACKAGED INVESTMENTS OF today are a continuation of the limited partnerships from days past. Limited partnerships got a bad name, so now they use other names, such as closed-in REITs, to make them more attractive. You will never hear the financial services industry use the term *packaged investment*, but that is what they are. Years from now, closed-end REITs will have a bad name, and the financial services industry will be selling packaged investments under a different name to the next generation of unsavvy investors. The investment results, however, will be the same.

Because these products have large sales percentages, there will always be advisors willing to sell them to unsavvy investors. They prey on investors who are afraid of losing money, making these out to be safer than they are. Years from now, packaged investments will still be out there. Not all advisors sell these investments to their customers.

I was once staying in a motel and I noticed that they had two security guards and a car. I couldn't stand not knowing why they had so much security, so I asked the desk clerk. I couldn't believe his answer, that the motel was a limited partnership and the general partners owned a security company. This is how investors are treated when they invest in products that are designed to take advantage of them. This is another example of The Doctor and The Cows.

Here are some easy ways to identify these products now or in the future:

They never show you a sales charge.

They promise or imply that you can get your money back in full in the future, if requested. If they promise that you will get your money back, remember that this promise is not backed up with any assets other than the investment itself. Many times, they will mention that they have the right of first refusal to buy you out. This is really worth nothing, but it sounds good.

The prospectus is very thick. If you did have enough time to read it and totally understand it, you would realize how much they make selling the investment and how much they charge managing the property. They charge more to manage the property since they are dealing with people who are unsavvy and wouldn't know the difference. A big institution would pay much less for property management because they would negotiate from a position of strength and knowledge. You the customer, who bought a product that was designed to overcharge you, are in a position of weakness.

Many times these packaged investments are associated with a company that is a household name. Take my advice and buy stock in the company that they are associated with instead. Just because a well-known company is renting your property does not make this a good investment for you.

In many cases your investment does not have a secondary market. The reason for this is your initial investment is only worth eighty-five cents on the dollar the day that you buy it, and the firm that sold you the packaged product doesn't want you to know that. They have an artificial value to make you believe that your investment is worth full price. Your account statement will never show you the value. Never invest in any security that you cannot look up and see the value or worth. If you want to know the value, the annual report will have a book value per share. Never sell an investment unless you know its value.

In some cases they won't have a surrender charge. They don't need a surrender charge if they take 15 percent off the top and tell you that it is worth full value.

HOW PENSION FUNDS AND INSURANCE COMPANIES INVEST THEIR MONEY

IF YOU ARE LOOKING for a good model for a conservative portfolio, then look at your company pension plan, the pension plan of a state that is not broke, or an insurance company's float (money from which they play claims). They generally invest conservatively in a mix of stocks, bonds, real estate, and cash. The funds are professionally managed at a fraction of the cost that you or I would pay for management. This model works for them, and it may be worth considering for you. Today's extremely low interest rates are not a good time to be in bonds. Use this model with a low cost, buy and hold approach.

NEVER

1. Buy an investment that has a surrender charge.
2. Buy an investment with an artificial value.
3. Buy an investment that hides the sales charges.

4. Buy an investment that you can't figure out the true cost of the fees and expenses.

5. Buy an investment that you cannot look up its value.

6. Believe that the annual expenses are the true annual costs of owning a mutual fund or annuity.

7. Invest in mutual funds unless you take the time to add up the annual fees and expenses, sales charges, management fees, 12B-1 fees, and additional expenses, in order to know the total cost of the fund.

8. Buy an investment product that has the ability to hide the true cost and overcharge you.

9. Panic sell during a correction.

10. Sell an investment without knowing its value.

11. Be too greedy when making investment decisions.

IF YOU DON'T WANT YOUR KIDS TO GET ALONG AFTER YOU ARE GONE

THE BEST WAY TO have a family that does not get along after you are gone is to put them in a family business together, own property together, or treat them unequally with money, now or after you are gone. If you can help it, never have your children own anything together. Groups tend to make better decisions with one exception: family members.

HE EVEN DIED IN 1974

DADDY HAD A FRIEND who he said had "done everything right". He was a successful farmer who had made a lot of money in stocks and bonds with the buy and hold approach. Buy and hold worked well in the past, and it works even better today because of ETFs. Financial Advisors are taught to bad mouth buy and hold, because it is not very profitable for them. They tried to teach me how to talk people out of buy and hold when I was an E F Hutton broker. Buy and hold has no annual expenses, and much less taxes. Daddy used to say that he did everything right, and that "he even died in 1974", the year the stock market had a 48 percent correction, saving his heirs a bundle on estate and inheritance taxes.

BEST MANAGER OUT OF MANY

DON'T LET AN ADVISOR sell you a managed account based on a managers past investment results. The trick that they use is to find the manager with the best results instead of the honest approach of disclosing the results of all of their managed accounts after fees and expenses. They are chasing winners, which is a losers game. Brokerage firms could easily disclose the investment results of all their managed accounts, but don't expect it. They would never do this since the investment results aren't all that great. I would never consider having a managed account unless I expected to make at least 3 percent above the index that I am trying to beat in order to cover the additional taxes and be worth my risk. Managed accounts are a fools game, lagging the indexes after fees and expenses, while costing the customer more in taxes.

There is something wrong about the financial services industry making more on my money than I make above the index. It's even worse when you pay the financial services industry lots of money to lag an index, which is the norm. If they could guarantee that they would beat the index over time or pay back the fees and expenses if they didn't, then it might be worth considering. That would be fair. Trying to beat the index is like gambling, since most investors who try don't do as well over time as the index they are trying to beat, while paying more in taxes on taxable accounts.

LAST DOLLAR

WHEN TAX PLANNING, ALWAYS ask your accountant what the last dollar cost you. If you take a big gain, the taxes might be low on the first part and then go up on a sliding scale to the last dollar. This will help you with planning. Always find out what the taxes will be before taking a large capital gain.

STICK BY THE RULES

ONE REASON WHY INDIVIDUAL investors might not do as well as professionals is that many times they don't stick by the rules. Never invest too much in one stock or industry. Mutual funds and money managers are required to limit exposure to one stock.

PARTNERSHIPS

IF YOU GO INTO a partnership, do it right. Get a buy/sale agreement with insurance to cover each partner. A good lawyer and insurance agent can help you with your planning. Daddy, who practiced law for thirty-five years, used to say that people would go into business thinking about how great things would be, and a few years later they would be dragging their ass in his office in trouble, much of which could have been avoided with proper planning. The worst cases were when they signed a contract with a big corporation without having it looked over by an attorney first.

LONG-TERM CARE INSURANCE

NEVER ATTEND A SEMINAR on long term care planning that is a front for selling long term care insurance.

Most financial advisors don't explain the options, other than purchasing insurance, to funding long term care. A salesperson will always sell you something as an answer to a problem instead of considering all of the options. Once again your interest is second to the financial services industry.

There are two reasons to purchase long term care insurance. The first reason is to be able to cover the expenses of the nursing home of choice or in home care. The second reason, which I question, is to protect your estate against the cost of long term care. Self insuring should be considered as an alternative to insurance. My mother bought a long term care policy against my advice, when she could have easily self insured. Remember that insurance is always a bad investment, only to be used when you cannot afford to take the risk.

Before spending several thousand dollars a year on a long term care policy, talk with an attorney that specializes in long term care planning. There are ways to move assets out of your name in order to protect your estate. Don't be cheap, spend money on the attorney instead of getting stuck in a supposedly free seminar that is designed to sell long term care insurance.

Many financial advisors will try to show you why you are in the net worth bracket that can't afford to self insure. Take their proposals and compound them at 7 percent for your life expectancy and you will have a good idea as to the true cost of the insurance policy (With the exception of rate increases, which is the norm.). Then see how much the benefit will be. A 3 year, 150 dollar per day policy for a couple age 55 with a 3 percent inflation rider and the ability to share the years costs 3,320 dollars per year. If you compound 1,660 for 25 years for the male and 1,660 for 28 years for the female at a modest 7 percent rate of return, you will have 275,724 dollars. This is a reasonable guess as to the true cost of the insurance. The maximum benefit in 25 years will be 687,806. The chances that you will max out your policy are slim. Divide the true cost of the premiums over your life expectancy into the maximum benefit, and you will see how bad of an investment long term care insurance is. Divide275,724 by 687,806 and you get 40 percent. Always do your own math instead of having a salesperson do it for you. Another way to look at the situation is that you are going to be paying 40 percent with the insurance, whether you use it or not.

Never buy insurance because it is a good investment. The insurance companies pay back 50 cents on the dollar. You buy insurance because you are unable to self insure. If you were rich enough, self insurance would be one of your best investments. All of the big corporations do it. The insurance companies may not be getting rich, but they rarely go broke. Long term care is a medical expense. All medical expenses over 7.5 percent are tax deductable. Your 401K, annuity, or other income can be used basically tax free to cover long term care expenses. That makes your 401K worth around 40 percent more if used to cover long term care expenses.

Unlike other insurance, don't shop for the cheapest long-term care insurance. Look at the companies that just had a rate increase, since this is the trend. The low-interest-rate environment that we are in is very costly to the insurance companies which have much of their reserves in short term fixed rate investments.

Many life insurance companies are now offering a long-term care rider on your life insurance, where you can use up your death benefit in a long-term care situation. These are only on permanent policies. You should check with your insurance carrier to see if this option is available to you on your current policy. I would always consider life insurance with a long term care rider as an alternative to long term care insurance because the life insurance is more competitive. The life insurance will not be subject to a rate increase.

My advice is to consider self insuring as an option. Always talk to an attorney who specializes in long term care before buying an expensive insurance policy. I doubt that any other financial books would recommend self insuring, since most are written by financial advisors who have sold long term care insurance.

SELF INSURED VS. NO INSURANCE

THERE IS A DIFFERENCE between self insuring and not having insurance, or not having adequate insurance. You plan on being self insured when you can afford to take the risk. Not having insurance, or not having adequate insurance is not a plan.

DON'T BE INSURANCE POOR

INVEST YOUR MONEY IN investments, instead of insurance, which is a poor investment. Insurance companies pay back around 50 cents on the dollar. They pay even less on long term policies.

"DON'T LEAVE YOUR 401K AT YOUR OLD JOB"

THE FINANCIAL SERVICES INDUSTRY makes a lot of money from you when you transfer your 401K. Your account will cost you more at a brokerage firm unless you invest in buy and hold stocks, or low-cost ETFs, which most advisors will try to talk you out of in favor of mutual funds or managed money. Moving your 401K to a brokerage firm can cost you more money on fees and expenses even if you are invested in the same mutual funds, since most 401K plans have a lower cost for mutual funds in their plans, and don't have the 1/4 percent advisory fee. If you are happy with your 401K plan, consider leaving it alone. Your former employer doesn't have control over it, the company that administers the 401K plan does.

PROFESSIONS THAT ARE BAD WITH MONEY

IF YOU ARE IN one of the professions that do poorly with their investments (you know who you are), don't join your peers. It is sad that so many people in certain professions who make plenty of money do so poorly with their investments. People in these careers tend to pay much more to the financial services industry than average and also make far less than average on their investments. They should never listen to financial advice from their peers. When choosing a financial advisor, they need to consider one who is realistic in expectations instead of those who promise or imply that they can beat the market. They should understand exactly what their advisors are making from their account and not let it get out of control. The main reason that certain professions are bad with money is that they try to outsmart the market, or ego. Egotistical investments, like absentee owned restaurants or resort property are proven ways to lose money.

HOW TO DEAL WITH YOUR FINANCIAL ADVISOR

YOU ARE THE CUSTOMER. You make the rules for handling your investments. Be cost conscious. This will not only save you money, but you will be in better investments. Buy and hold works; it always did. Never have an advisor who tries to talk you out of buy and hold. Why would anyone want an advisor that gives bad advice? Never pay an annual fee that is a percentage of your account. Don't be fooled into believing that they are going to make you so much more over time on your investments that the advisory fees or the 2 percent that mutual funds really cost won't matter. Look at your IRS Form 1099. If you have a lot of capital gains from your investments, then you are paying much more in taxes than if you were a buy and hold investor. Add the unnecessary taxes to the unnecessary management fees and expenses, and compound the reduced rate of return over a number of years to see for yourself how much less you will have in your old age.

DON'T NEED A FINANCIAL ADVISOR

I AM A FORMER financial advisor and I still have an advisor in order to keep me out of trouble. Very few people are able to do things on their own without making mistakes that end up being more costly than having an advisor. Having a greedy advisor however, is much worse than having no advisor at all.

SOCIAL SECURITY

WHATEVER OPTION YOU CHOSE as to when you take Social Security retirement, is actuarially the same amount of money. If you take the early retirement option, a nonworking spouse will be greatly penalized.

I don't like hearing that Social Security will not be around in the future. It will be around, but in order for the system to survive, benefits will have to be reduced and/or payments will need to increase, or both. The longer Congress puts off dealing with Social Security, the more costly the problem will be. We need to demand Social Security reform sooner instead of later.

Beware of seminars that imply that they can show you how to get much more from Social Security.

GENEROSITY

DON'T EXPECT YOUR CHILDREN to carry on your acts of generosity. Make sure that important acts of generosity are taken care of before you die. That doesn't mean trust them to your children. It's temping for a child to forget an obligation in order to keep the monies for themselves.

EXPECTATIONS

ONE WAY TO LOSE money in the market is to start with expectations that are too high. Many financial advisors imply that your investments will do much better with them, as if only losers match the S&P 500. Never leave an advisor for one that promises more. Choose the advisor that is realistic and promises less.

THROWING DARTS

THROWING DARTS IN ORDER to pick stocks does have an advantage over selecting stocks, in that emotion does not influence your decision. Throwing darts might have an advantage over throwing away 2 percent a year on mutual fund fees and expenses. I am not saying that you should throw darts in order to select stocks, but you do need to understand how your emotions will lead you to buy companies when they are high, and sell companies when they are low. Your emotions can lose money in the stock market.

PEOPLE WHO ALWAYS GET IN THE MARKET AT THE HIGH

EVERY TIME THAT THE market gets heated, some of the people who never invest in the stock market get in. They wouldn't dare invest during a correction, the best time to buy, because of the uncertainty. These investors are much more prone to dump their stocks or mutual funds on the worst day, during a correction.

HEATED STOCK MARKET

JOE KENNEDY SAID IN 1929 before the crash "When the time comes that a shoeshine boy knows as much as I do about what is going on in the stock market... it's time for me to get out." The best time to buy is during times of uncertainty, when the market is off. Nobody can pick the high or low. Don't try

Sins of the Father, Ronald Kessler, Warner Books, New York, 1996, page 82

WHEN TO SELL

KNOWING WHEN TO SELL is difficult. A proven time not to sell is during a correction. A smart investor has a plan not to panic sell before corrections occur. Buy and hold investors have an advantage of not having to figure out when to sell unlike those who trade often.

MAIL BOX

I HATE WALKING OUT to my mail box in anticipation of getting a check only to be disappointed. With rental property that's the way things are. Rental property is not for everyone.

BASIS

ONE RECORD THAT YOU must keep is the cost basis on your investments. Today, brokerage firms keep this information for you. Check to make sure that your old accounts include the basis. If you give an investment to someone, the receiver gets your basis which they must keep up with. The receiver must pay taxes on a gain, but they cannot write off a loss. Your heirs get a stepped-up basis (updated). They start over and don't have to keep up with old records pertaining to basis. Heirs must save the inventory of an inherited estate because it has the cost basis for their securities and real estate.

A REALLY BAD INVESTMENT, LIDIGATION

DADDY, WHO PRACTICED LAW for 35 years used to say " If people were reasonable, I wouldn't have a job."

PORTFOLIO OF CORE STOCKS

CORE STOCKS ARE COMPANIES that are leaders in their industries. Investing in core stocks is a conservative way to invest for the long term and have higher dividends and less volatility than the market. My core stock portfolio held up much better than the S&P 500 in 2009, but it didn't do as well in the recovery. If you look up the largest holdings of most mutual funds, you will find core stocks. Go to the library and look through the Value Line at all the industries, or find an advisor willing to do this with you. Individual stocks are only suitable for those who are able to keep up with them. Look for companies that pay good dividends that have a history of increased earnings and dividends. Stocks that pay good dividends tend to hold up better in bear markets. Don't be too greedy chasing dividends. If the dividends are too high, something could be wrong. At the time of this book, there are many blue chip companies that pay between 3 and 4 percent. Some utilities and oil companies are paying around 5 percent.

PLAY MONEY

DADDY CALLED OWNER FINANCING "play money". Those who could not get their price for a business or real estate would settle for owner financing instead of selling it for what it was really worth. In thirty-five years of practicing law, he saw many owner financing deals go south. Owner financing should be a last resort, used to sell properties or businesses that cannot be sold any other way.

YOUR FRIENDS AT THE BANK

THE LAST TIME INTEREST rates went up, your friends at the bank sent letters to their customers offering to buy back their mortgages at a discount. They didn't do this because they were generous; they did it because the mortgage companies paid them to help sell off their low interest loans. Your mortgage was worth more to them than the discount that they were offering to you. The customers who did this were surprised when they received an IRS Form 1099 at the end of the year, because forgiveness of debt is a taxable event. The next time interest rates go up sharply, you can be sure that the banks will pull this trick out of the bag.

LEARN FROM OTHERS MISTAKES

THE BEST WAY TO learn is from mistakes. Most people, including myself, tend to learn more from their own mistakes than from others. Daddy saw a lot of mistakes practicing law. My accountant has also seen many mistakes. Lawyers and accountants give advice that will help keep you out of trouble, because part of their job is getting people out of trouble.

PICK FIVE SHOW-OFFS IN YOUR TOWN

IF YOU PICK FIVE show offs in your town and wait ten years, chances are good that at least one of them will go broke. Many people are surprised because they thought that the person had an unlimited supply of money. Don't be one of the people in town who end up with a worthless note.

WHERE ARE THE REAL BROKERS

TODAY'S FINANCIAL ADVISORS HAVE it made. The most important thing they do is help you with asset allocation while putting you in captive investments. Whatever happened to the real stockbrokers that recommended individual stocks and bonds and built a reputation on their advice? In the past, they never charged annual fees. All of this overpriced crap that we have today is what's paying for us to have too many financial advisors. The reason that so many companies are getting into the financial service industry today is because it's so profitable, not because they are good at it.

"Newfangled brokers have many things besides stocks to sell, including annuities, limited partnerships, tax shelters, insurance policies, CDs, bond funds, and stock funds. They must understand all of these 'products' at least well enough to make the pitch. They have neither the time nor the inclination to track the utilities or the retailers or the auto sector, and since few clients are invested in individual stocks, there's little demand for their stock picking advice. Anyway, the broker's biggest commissions are made elsewhere, on mutual funds, underwritings, and in the options game."[14]

Peter Lynch, Beating the Street, Simon and Schuster, New York, 1993, page 25

CORPORATE BONDS

NEVER BUY BOND MUTUAL funds, because the fees and sales charges eat up much of the return. Buy the real thing, the bonds, or low cost ETFs. Some mutual bond funds pay more than the bonds themselves, but do not be impressed. The trick that they are using is leverage. Leveraged bond funds are more risky. Leveraged bond mutual funds look really good until interest rates rise.

MUNICIPAL BONDS

ON SMALL AMOUNTS, CONSIDER ETFs. On larger amounts, have your advisor call the bond desk or deal directly with a municipal bond broker in order to build a portfolio for your needs. Never buy mutual funds or unit trusts for bonds because the fees and expenses eat up your returns.

AM I BEING TOO GREEDY?

BEFORE MAKING ANY INVESTMENT, always ask yourself if you are being too greedy. Pay more attention to how much you could lose rather than how much you could make. Do not invest in stocks if you think you might panic and sell during a major correction.

HOW TO FIND THE LOW

TWO WAYS TO FIND the low on stocks or the market is to panic sell during a correction or have a margin call. "Don't own any stock that would cause you to panic and dump your shares if the price falls by 50 percent."

James Pardoe, How Buffet Does It, McGraw Hill, New York, 2005, page 19

OTHER PEOPLES HANDS

WHEN OTHER PEOPLE HAVE their hands on your money, they will take their share. The longer their hands are on your money, the more they feel they deserve. This is why I don't own any captive investments. I always know exactly what my investments cost. You should also.

EVERYBODY AND THEIR BROTHER OR SISTER IN THE FINANCIAL SERVICES INDUSTRY

IF YOUR GENERAL INSURANCE agent is capable to serve as your financial advisor, then that is proof that you are capable of managing your investments yourself. One captive insurance company, which is already too high for insurance, charges seventy-six basis points for their S&P 500 ETF instead of five basis points for the same ETF at Vanguard. It would take over fifteen years at Vanguard to equal one year of their expenses.

There are way more financial advisors today than in the 1980s when I was in the business. Everybody and their brother or sister are getting in the financial services industry because it is so profitable, not because they are good at it. If the public wasn't so willing to overpay for financial services, things would be better.

MANAGED MONEY

A FINANCIAL ADVISOR'S DREAM is to have all of their high net worth clients in managed money. The managed accounts must beat the market by enough to cover the fees and expenses, and make up for the additional taxes incurred by account turnover in order for you to break even. Managed money is a fools game.

Investors would be much better off with a buy and hold approach with low cost ETFs or core stocks.

Do not let an advisor talk you into" firing the manager "and staying in the program with a different manager if your results didn't beat the index. They can always find a manager with a high performance history to sell you. Try a broad-based ETF for the next five years instead. Notice how much less capital gains are on your IRS Form 1099 with a broad based ETF. Also notice that you will have to pay more taxes on dividends since they are not being offset by management fees and expenses, which is a good thing. Ask your accountant how much taxes you are saving with the ETF. I would like to hear some of the things that the financial advisors might say in order to convince you to stay in managed money for comedy in my next book. Don't let an advisor make you feel guilty for leaving a program that is not in your best interest.

Before being sold any managed money program, have the advisor sign an agreement that they will put you in low-cost ETFs at no charge, and without any begging, if the managed account doesn't outperform the index by a large enough margin to cover your taxes and be worth your trouble after 5 years(a reasonable time to compare the managed account to the ETF).

If you must try the managed account, consider putting half of your investment in a low cost broad based ETF without any annual fees or expenses, and the other half in the managed account. Every year credit which ever account ends up costing you less in taxes. After 5 years close the loosing account and move the money into the winning account.

WHEN TO CONVERT TO A ROTH

CONSIDER CONVERTING YOUR IRA or 401K to a Roth. You pay the taxes now, and the account will be tax-free in the future. A conversion may not be advantageous if you plan to withdraw the money in a few years, or if you are in a higher tax bracket than you will be in retirement. The money must be in the account for five years in order to withdraw the principal without a penalty before age 59 1/2. A good time to convert is when you think that the market is low, or if you have a year that you are in a low tax bracket. You can convert part of your account each year in order to reduce taxes. If you convert, and the value of your account decreases considerably, you have until October 15 the following year to nullify your conversion.

Nondeductible IRAs should always be converted, since the basis can be converted with no taxes. With a Roth you do not have to receive distributions at age seventy and a half. Many financial websites help you decide if and how much to convert.

Here is a scenario in which a conversion would be a waste: If my wife or I were in a long-term care situation, my 401K, IRA, or any other income could be used tax-free to cover medical expenses. All medical expenses exceeding 7.5 percent of income are tax deductable.

WHEN TO ROTH INSTEAD OF PRE- TAX CONTRIBUTIONS

THERE ARE TWO THINGS to consider when deciding whether to put pre tax or after tax money into a retirement account: your current tax bracket verses your retirement tax bracket, and the number of years before you withdraw the money. Young people should consider a Roth 401K or Roth IRA even if they make smaller contributions, because of the longer the time period, especially if they are in the 15 percent federal income tax bracket. It would not be smart to defer taxes at 15 percent in order to pay 28 percent in retirement with a traditional 401K or IRA . Also, consider the Roth as an estate planning tool. Your heirs can continue the Roth, but are required to receive distributions based on their life expectancy free of taxes.

THEY ARE TREATING PEOPLE LIKE IDIOTS AT THE BANK

A FRIEND OF MINE told me this story recently, and I thought that it was a good example of the decline of the financial services industry. He had a CD at the bank coming due, and the bank kept bothering him about meeting with their financial advisor. He went to the appointment, and while he was waiting outside of the door, he was able to overhear the advisor talking to a couple. The advisor asked the couple how would they like to own stock in McDonalds and Coke, and then he started pushing a mutual fund, never mentioning the fees and expenses.

NONPROFITS

FOR SOME REASON NONPROFITS spend much more than they should on management fees. Apparently, the directors would rather not be held responsible for investment decisions. If you are on a board of a charity, consider low-cost investment options. Don't expect financial advisors to come to a meeting in order to pitch low-cost alternatives. Save on fees and expenses, and use the savings for the benefit of the church or charity. I look at how well my church and charities control their expenses. I don't appreciate being asked for money from an organization that can afford to pay 1 1/2 to 2 percent a year in investment advisory fees when there are so many quality low-cost options available.

MAKE YOUR OWN MUTUAL FUND

UNCLE TOM USED TO say, "Make your own mutual fund. Buy an assortment of quality stocks that pay good dividends and hold them for the long term." Stocks that have a history of increasing dividends have outperformed the market over time. Consider core stocks (leaders in their industries). A good way to find good companies to invest in is to look at holdings of mutual funds or the Value Line. The Value Line, which is usually at your library, follows around 2,000 companies.

Build a portfolio of core stocks with an advisor, or by yourself. Keep it simple. Only invest in stocks that you are prepared to hold for the long term. This is not for you, if you think that you might panic and sell during a correction. My retirement is mostly in core stocks that pay good dividends, which I reinvest. My portfolio may not do as well as the S&P 500 in good times, but it holds up much better during corrections.

It's funny that someone who has not kept up with the S&P 500 has written a book about how to invest your money. Not keeping up with the S&P 500 is something that I have in common with the financial services industry. My portfolio held up much better than the S&P 500 in 2009 When the next correction occurs, and it will, my portfolio will hold up much better than the market again. If beating the S&P 500 over a long period of time is your goal, all you have to do is buy a low cost, broader based ETF than the S&P 500 and hold on to it. If your index has more midcap, small cap, and foreign stocks, then you will have more volatility and more long term potential returns (more risk should equal more returns over time). You will also have less taxes and headaches with the ETF.

I tend to make the same mistakes that most investors make. I try not to get excited when the market is high, and since I am already fully invested I am unable to buy during corrections, but I rarely sell. One exception would be to sell at a loss and buy a similar stock that is equally beat up in order to create a tax loss. I, like everybody, miss the obvious. Why did I not load up on healthcare when Clinton's health reform failed? It was a half-price sale on an industry that could do nothing but go up. Why did I not load up on oil stocks when gas was $1.25 a gallon? If you had asked me what the price of gas was going to be in the future, I would have said much higher. The next time that we have a corporate executive resign to become president or vice president, you can bet that I will load up on their stock.

25.65 PERCENT IN EXPENSES OVER TEN YEARS TO UNDERPERFORM AN INDEX

I WAS LOOKING OVER an account recently that was invested in mutual funds. It had a popular mutual fund which had sales charges and expenses of 15.65 percent over the past ten years. That did not include the statement of additional expenses or the management fee, which was around 1 percent a year, making the total cost 25.65 percent. During this time, it failed to perform as well as the indexes that were closest to their objectives. Their institutional shares, because of no sales charge and lower annual expenses did better, but they lagged the index also. There is something wrong with paying that kind of money to underperform an index, which happens most of the time with mutual funds. At least it wasn't a taxable account, or the results would have been worse.

MAKING BAD INVESTMENT DECISIONS IN ORDER TO SAVE ON TAXES

YEARS AGO, BEFORE CAPITAL gains tax were getting ready to end, Daddy had a track of pine timber that was ready to cut. Everybody in the county was selling their timber in order to get the capital gains. He noticed that there weren't any mature tracts of pine timber left in the county. He waited two years, and doubled the appraisal on the timber. After paying ordinary taxes, he was still far ahead.

Always consider taxes when making investment decisions. Don't ever buy packaged investments because of potential tax savings.

THE GOVERMENT WILL NEED MORE MONEY IN THE FUTURE

THE FEDERAL AND STATE governments will need more money in the future. Buy and hold investors have always paid less in taxes than the accounts that trade often. That will not change.

THE POWER OF DEFFERED INCOME

"THE POWER OF DEFERRED income" is a slogan created by a greedy industry to sell you highly overpriced annuities that are in most cases tax inefficient.

THE BOYS AT JACKASS

I TOLD MY SON that if you study hard, you probably won't make as much money as the boys on Jackass. However, if you follow my investment advice, you will probably end up much better off financially.

One reason why many highly paid famous people end up in financial trouble is that they trust others to handle their finances. Another reason is that they piss the money away, since they think it will never end. The third reason is egotistical investments like absentee-owned restaurants.

HOUSE VS. CONDO

DON'T GET A CONDO in order to save a little money on landscaping and exterior maintenance. Look at the assessment history and talk to owners about possible future assessments. In many cases condo fees and assessments can be more costly than home ownership. Many times associations like to spend too much money A friend told me that if you show me a condo manager, I will show you someone that is getting their yard landscaped for free. A home, if you are able to afford it has advantages over a condo or townhouse.

HOW COULD THEY HIDE MY 401K FEES FOR EIGHTEEN YEARS WITHOUT ME KNOWING?

I LOOK OVER MY statements regularly, and I have never seen an annual fee on my 401K. I started thinking about it while writing this book, and I asked. I have been paying 50 dollars a year on each account in annual fees. If I looked a hell of a lot more, I still could not have found it. I was told that the only way to find it is to look for the movement of monies the month in which it is paid. It's not the cost that upsets me, it's the way that it is hidden.

Do you have any idea how much your 401K is costing you? Most people don't.

DON'T TAKE NO FOR AN ANSWER

YEARS AGO, WHEN I was in New York training to be a stock-broker, we had an instructor who was teaching us not take no for an answer. One day he was calling prospects trying to sell a utility stock, when he reached a person who said that they already had too much of that stock. He put them on hold, grabbed a Value Line, and recommended that they sell 1,000 shares since they had too much of that stock, and buy 1,000 shares of the utility on the next page. This is an example of how financial advisors are trained to sell first, and take care of customers second.

4 PERCENT RATE OF RETURN

FOR PLANNING PURPOSES, USE a 4 percent rate of return if you want to ensure that you will not deplete your nest egg. (Recently, this has been challenged because interest rates are so low.) If you had retired before the market drop in 1974, 4.4 percent a year would have been the most that you would have been able to have taken and still recovered with a balanced account. The drop and slow recovery in 1974 was the worst in our history. The market will likely do 7 percent over time, but if you happen to retire be-fore a major correction, it would be better to play it safe. Today, people are living thirty years or more into their retirement. An account that would deplete their savings over thirty years would yield very little more than an account that was designed to last.

TRAVEL

I UNDERSTAND THAT TRAVEL tips aren't usually found in a book about investments. However, I have been fortunate to have spent six months travelling overseas and have a few pointers on how to get the most out of travel.

BIGGEST TRAVEL MISTAKES

1. Covering too much distance
2. Over packing
3. Tourist traps
4. Traveling with too large of a group

TRAVEL TIPS

GET A CREDIT CARD that doesn't charge the typical 3 percent exchange fee. It will be mentioned in the fine print section of your credit card information. Always take out large amounts at ATMs since each international transaction costs $5. Some banks and credit unions will wave a few ATM fees per month. Getting money before going overseas can cost over 6 percent in exchange fees at the airport; however, they pay a decent price on arrival. It is not cheap to order foreign money from the banks. Save your foreign money and sell it to friends who are going on vacation at cost.

Try to go slightly off-season. You will save on airfare, accommodations, and rental cars. June or September is off-season in Europe. It will be much less crowded than July or August.

Avoid packaged vacations.

Rent cottages.

Four people in a rental car is cheaper than travelling by train. If your vacation is mostly visiting cities, then the train makes more sense.

Go to the countryside.

Consider traveling off-season with a car and no itinerary.

Study up on where you are going.

If you must do laundry, go to a campground. Your vacation is too expensive to spend in a Laundromat.

Know your cost per day.

If you are travelling and rooms are hard to find, let the tourist office find one for you in order to save time and aggravation.

Most airlines and resorts will honor a lower price if it occurs after you made your reservations. It is up to you to inform them.

It is easier to travel speaking only English every year. English is the language of diplomacy, aviation, and computers. It is, however, more difficult to get by speaking English in the countryside and away from the tourist areas.

If you really want to get to know a country, look up a travel itinerary of a packaged vacation and try as much as possible to deviate from it. Most people who go on packaged vacations go to the same places. I've never heard of anyone who travelled on their own complain about a vacation.

Ireland would be a nice trip for those who are taking their first independent vacation. Shannon airport is in the country, making it easy to drive to the hotel or cottage. The Irish are extremely friendly. I would rent a car with automatic transmission, since driving on the left side of the road is difficult enough without having to shift gears with your left hand. Be careful when crossing the street, and look to the right. Winston Churchill was hit by a car in New York City by looking right instead of left.

The criminals are planning ahead for the tourist season. You should be planning on them as well.

When overseas, you are representing your country. The rest of the world has different views on things than we do. Know your current events.

GLOSSARY

ALTERNATIVE MINIMUM TAX (AMT): A 28 percent tax rate that you qualify for if you have too many tax breaks, such as too much dividends or capital gains. Home mortgage and charitable deductions do not put you in AMT.

BALANCED ACCOUNT: 60 PERCENT bonds or cash equivalents and 40 percent stocks

BASIS: YOUR COST OF AN INVESTMENT FOR TAX PURPOSES.

BASIS POINT: 1 percent of a percent; e.g., 100 basis points equals 1 percent

CAPITAL GAINS: A preferred tax rate on assets sold that were held for over a year with a rate of 0, 15, or 20 percent, depending on your ordinary tax rate. Once you get into AMT your tax rate jumps to 28 percent.

CAPTIVE INVESTMENTS: Investments where your assets are held by a custodian, usually with fees and expenses that you would not be paying if you owned the assets outright.

CLIFFORD TRUST: A trust where you put in an asset that someone else receives the income from. It is used when the receiver is in a much lower tax bracket. The Clifford trust must be for a period of at least 10 years, and must be set up by an attorney.

CORE STOCKS: Stocks of large companies that are leaders in their industries. Core stocks usually pay better dividends and have less volatility, but also have less upside potential than the market.

DEDUCTABLE: The amount you must pay first before your insurance policy pays on claims

DIVIDEND TAX RATES: 0, 15, or 20 percent on qualified stocks until you get into AMT, which is 28 percent

ETF: A fund that trades like a stock and holds an unmanaged portfolio that is based on an index

LOW COST MUTUAL FUND: A mutual fund that has no sales charges, and has low management fees.

PERMANENT LIFE INSURANCE: Whole life or universal life insurance

STEPPED UP BASIS: When someone inherits anything of value the new cost basis is the date of death or 6 months after. The estate can only use one date. This can be a huge tax advantage.

UNIT TRUST: A structure that holds stocks and bonds in a diversified portfolio that costs the customer considerably more than if they owned the stocks and bonds outright.

www.ingramcontent.com/pod-product-compliance
Lightning Source LLC
Chambersburg PA
CBHW051728170526
45167CB00002B/842